# Latino and Latina Leaders

## of the

## 21st Century:

## Ordinary Beginnings, Extraordinary Outcomes

By Kay (Kayla) S. García

Oregon State University

Floricanto

Floricanto Press
7177 Walnut Canyon Rd.
Moorpark, California 93021
(415) 793-2662
www. Floricantopress. Com
ISBN-10: 1-888205-48-2
ISBN-13: 978-1-888205-48-0
*"Por nuestra cultura hablarán nuestros libros. Our books shall speak for our culture."*
Roberto Cabello-Argandoña, Editor
Assistant Editor, Yasmeen Namazie
Front and back covers by Deann García

Latino and Latina Leaders of the 21st Century

This book is dedicated to my husband, Tracy Rupp, with love and appreciation for all of his help and encouragement.

I also dedicate this book to my daughter Verona García, my son Bill García, my daughter-in-law Deann García, and my grandchildren: Avilana, Solaris and Marazul Tafolla-García.

# Table of Contents

Kay (Kayla) S. García

## Acknowledgments

This book was made possible because of a research grant from the School of Language, Culture and Society at Oregon State University (OSU), faculty release time and sabbatical leave granted by OSU, and support from the Center for the Humanities at OSU.

I am very grateful for the guidance and encouragement provided by Joseph Krause, Professor of French at OSU.

I wish to thank my husband, Tracy A. Rupp, for his important editing suggestions, his patience, and his belief in me.

I appreciate the careful editing done by Nancy Barbour, writing advisor for the School of Language, Culture and Society at OSU.

I am thankful for the help and feedback provided by the following people: Susana Rivera-Mills, Associate Dean of the College of Liberal Arts, OSU; Susan Shaw, Director of the School of Language, Culture and Society, OSU; David Robinson, Director of the Center for the Humanities, OSU; Wendy Madar, Associate Director of the Center for the Humanities, OSU; Alison Ruch, former office coordinator at the Center for the Humanities, OSU; Erlinda Gonzales-Berry, Director of Casa Latinos Unidos de Benton County; Karen Svenson, former teacher in Eugene, Oregon, School District; Nabil Boudraa, Associate Professor of French, OSU; Ruth Vondracek, head of the Reference Department at the OSU Valley Library; Richard Orozco, Assistant Professor of Education, University of Arizona South.

I wish to recognize all of the students who participated in my Latino Heroes class for their help in choosing which leaders to include in this book. I am particularly grateful to the following graduate students for their carefully annotated bibliographies: Geraldine Casimiro, Diana Kinross, Abby McArthur, Rory McNulty,

## Latino and Latina Leaders

Eder Mondragón, Maralisa Morales, Breann Mudrick, Michelle Ofelt, Joanna Pardue, Hilda Pereyó, Jill Reece, Rebecca Rung, Bárbara Tóvar Tello, Elena Valdés-Chavarría.

# Terms and Acronyms

## Terms

**Chicana/Chicano:** a term that refers to people of Mexican descent who are living in the United States. Ending in *a*, the word refers to a female person. Ending in *o*, the word refers to a male, but it is sometimes used generically to refer to both males and females, as in "Chicano Studies." Plural: Chicanas, Chicanos.

**Hispanic:** a term that refers to people who live in the United States and are descended from people who speak Spanish. Although this term is used frequently, some people object to the use of this term, and they prefer to be called Latinos.

**Latin American:** a person originating from Latin America who has lived in that area and identifies more with that region than with a new place of residence. Many Latin Americans identify themselves by their individual country rather than by the region.

**Latina/Latino:** a term that refers to people who live in the United States and are descended from people who speak Spanish. Ending in *a*, the word refers to a female person. Ending in *o*, the word refers to a male, but it is sometimes used generically to refer to both males and females, as in "Latino Studies." Plural: Latinas, Latinos.

**Latin@:** an abbreviated way to say "Latino and Latina." Plural: Latin@s.

**Xicanisma:** a term utilized by Ana Castillo in her work *Massacre of the Dreamers* (1994) to refer to Chicana feminism. By extension, Xicana refers to a Chicana feminist. This term has been used by other Chicana writers, such as Gloria Anzaldúa, Norma Alarcón, and

Cherríe Moraga, with slightly different meanings and associations.

### Acronyms:

**LGBTQ:** Lesbian, Gay, Bisexual, Transgender, and Queer (or Questioning), a community that is still referred to as LGBT by some people.

**PRI:** Partido Revolucionario Institucional (Institutional Revolutionary Party), the political party that ruled Mexico from 1929 to 2000 (with two name changes). After a hiatus of 12 years, the PRI won back the presidency in 2012.

**UFW:** United Farmworkers Union, an organization created by Dolores Huerta and César Chávez in 1962 (with two name changes).

## Introduction

Latino issues are everybody's issues. In Sandra Cisneros' story *Have You Seen Marie?*, a character called "River" merges with all the waterways, lakes, and oceans of the world, "washing away the dead... bringing new life, the salty and the sweet, mixing with everything, everything, everything, everything." Issues of concern to Latinos are like this river, since they are intertwined with every aspect of our society, and the advances made by Latinos have had multiple effects on our nation. Due to efforts by Latino activists, progress has been made in our social, legal, political and educational systems, as well as in protections for workers and consumers. Some of these improvements are obvious. For example, the boycotts and demonstrations organized by United Farm Workers (UFW) brought about better working conditions for agricultural laborers, including regulation of pesticides and access to toilets, soap and water near the fields. Thus, our nation's food supply became healthier because of improved sanitation and a reduction in the worst chemicals sprayed on produce.

Another observable advancement has occurred in the area of immigration reform, due in part to the efforts of Latino politicians, judges, and advocates. The 2012 Deferred Action for Childhood Arrivals program improved the status of immigrants brought to this country as children, allowing them to study and work in the United States for renewable two-year periods. In 2013, some progress has been made toward a comprehensive reform that would improve the circumstances of undocumented immigrants and provide a stable workforce for industry, agriculture, and services.

In a manner less evident to the public, Latino activists have promoted the rights of minorities, poor people, women, the LGBTQ community, crime victims, defendants, and speakers of other languages. Latino educators have cultivated awareness of the benefits of diversity, social activism, and bilingual education. Latino volunteers at outreach centers have helped people connect to communities and services. Latina authors have raised consciousness and promoted the rights of their own communities and of all women. The ripple effects of all of these contributions are significant, since by improving the life of one person you can improve the condition of the entire family, then of the community, and eventually of the nation.

The term *Latino* does not refer to race, but to ethnicity, and it encompasses many different identities and cultures. Although most Latinos speak Spanish or descend from Spanish speakers, some of them have ancestors from European countries other than Spain. Many Latinos are related to one or more of the numerous indigenous and African communities represented in the Americas. Moreover, there are Latinos with Jewish, Arabic, or Asian heritage. With this book I would like to honor Latinos and Latinas of all colors and backgrounds. (See the "Terms and Acronyms" page for more information on terminology.)

All the leaders portrayed in this volume are currently active. They have had ordinary or even humble beginnings and have overcome adversity in many forms. Serving as representatives and role models for their communities, these individuals have set precedents, built legacies, and paved the way for future generations. All of them are proud of their heritage and remain connected to the Latino community. They are proof that one can effect change in any setting, and at all levels, since they include people who work in local, state, national and international organizations. In this book I analyze what factors made it possible for these leaders to succeed, how they overcame seemingly insurmountable obstacles, and what lessons can be learned from their experiences. I hope to inspire future activists, as well as to inform others about some noteworthy Latinos in our area and throughout the United States.

I have chosen to focus on positive aspects of these leaders and of the Latino community in general, as a counterbalance to the negative news that dominates our mass media. However, I have not whitewashed these stories. All of these leaders are ordinary human beings, complete with flaws, but somehow they have managed to channel their energies in such a way that they have achieved extraordinary outcomes in their lifetime.

My own perspective is that of a natural ally to Latinos. I lived in Mexico for many years, and I have interacted with Latino communities in the United States for decades. I have taught hundreds of students to speak Spanish and to appreciate Latino and Latin American culture. I am related to some Latinos, even though I have no Spanish-speaking ancestors. Therefore, I am careful to use the third person when speaking of Latinos, and I have made a concerted effort to let them speak for themselves as much as possible by using quotes or by paraphrasing their ideas.

In the first five chapters of this book, I present detailed stories of individuals: Sonia Sotomayor, Supreme Court justice; Dolores Huerta, co-founder of the United Farm Workers union; Jorge Ramos, news anchor and advocate for immigrants; John Haroldson, district attorney, and his wife María Chávez-Haroldson, leadership facilitator; and Sandra Cisneros, author and activist. My sixth chapter presents a wide variety of Latino leaders in different fields, who have made connections to each other and to various causes. This final chapter will help convince the reader that Latino issues are connected to everything, everything, everything, everything.

## Sonia Sotomayor

## Chapter One

## Sonia Sotomayor: First Latina on the Supreme Court

"My biggest challenge has been dealing with other people's expectations, and having fun proving them wrong."

--Sonia Sotomayor

"My family showed me by their example how wonderful and vibrant life is and how wonderful and magical it is to have a Latina soul."

--Sonia Sotomayor

Sonia Sotomayor is a courageous and charismatic Latina who loves to dance salsa, sing karaoke, and root for the New York Yankees. As Assistant District Attorney she accompanied detectives into dangerous crime scenes, and as a corporate lawyer she rushed into warehouses on raids of counterfeiting operations. As a judge she has not been intimidated by powerful bullies nor swayed by personal interests, and she has maintained her integrity and faith in the rule of law. She is an influential role model who has overcome medical, professional, and societal obstacles and has set precedents at every level of her profession. She often expresses her strong attachment to the Latino community, and her profound gratitude toward her mother and grandmother. Since her first day as Associate Justice of the U.S. Supreme Court, Sonia[1] has played a very active role on the bench, asking questions and expressing strong arguments both in favor and against majority opinions. When she was nominated for this position, she faced a

---

1 I ask Sonia's and the reader's forgiveness for the use of her first name. It is my attempt to get close to my subject, and to help the reader identify with her.

media storm of opposition and doubts about her ability. At one point, she considered withdrawing from the confirmation process because of the lack of privacy and time for family and friends, but a colleague told her that it was not only important to her, it was important to all the young people of color who could have more faith in their dreams if she were on the Supreme Court.[2] Sonia took this observation seriously, since she knew how it felt to have no role models for her profession of choice: as she was coming of age, there were no Latina women on televised courtroom dramas, university faculty, at the DA's office, in private practice, nor on the federal bench. It might have been easier for her if she had found role models that looked like her and with whom she could identify. Maybe she wouldn't have doubted herself so much; but in spite of her doubts she persisted, and her story is one of hard work, dedication to her studies, perseverance, and integrity.

This is a serious story, but it is not devoid of humor. Sonia has been parodied on "Saturday Night Live," "Stand Up Comedy," and several other televised programs as well as countless YouTube videos, and many of these parodies point out aspects of her character that she is able to laugh about herself. However, the parody that best captured her playful spirit, which is usually cloaked by conservative suits or judicial robes, was the tango between impersonators of Sonia and her Supreme Court colleague Antonin Scalia on "The Vic and Paul Show." The pair danced a lively tango, singing and using gavels as castanets, trying to lure each other either to the left or to the right. Prophetically perhaps, they ended with a dramatic flourish in the center of the stage.[3]

---

2 Unless otherwise noted, biographical information comes from the books by Felix, Gitlin, and Greene, listed in the Bibliography, and/or from Sonia's memoir. Only direct quotes from these sources will be noted hereafter.

3 "Tango Sotomayor."

## Early years: A path through the darkness

In Sonia's memoir, *My Beloved World* (2013), she reveals some of the darker aspects of her childhood, such as being "walloped" at home, and being hit by teachers and classmates at school. Her father's alcoholism and her mother's chilly neglect also contributed to Sonia's misery. "[However,] I did have sources of great happiness," she insists, "and these bred in me an optimism that proved stronger than any adversity."[4] Her self-confidence was bolstered by the love and respect of her grandmother, *Abuelita*, who organized family gatherings and performed séances in which a spirit guide called Madame Sandorí spoke with a Jamaican accent. As an adult, Sonia has reconciled with her mother and recognized the value of her example. In almost every speech, Sonia gives thanks to her mother, who is often in the audience, and whose work ethic and belief in her children's potential inspired both Sonia and her brother Juan to excel.

Sonia's mother, Celina Baez Sotomayor, was born into oppressive poverty in Puerto Rico, where workers did hard labor for 12 cents a day. Her ticket out of that dead end was a job with the Women's Army Corps (WAC) during World War II, which brought her to New York. After the war she obtained her GED, worked as a phone operator, and eventually earned a nurse's license. Sonia's father, Juan Luis Sotomayor, also migrated from Puerto Rico to New York, where he found a job at a tool-and-die factory. Even though he did not speak English and had only a third-grade education, he was able to find work that paid much better than what he could have found on the island. In 1946, Celina and Juan married and settled into a tenement in the South Bronx. Sonia was born in 1954 and

---

4 Sotomayor vii.

her younger brother, Juan Luis Jr., was born a few years later.

When Sonia was seven months old, she learned how to walk and run on the same day. Her frenzied activity earned her the nickname "*Aji*" (Hot Pepper), and she often had to be rushed to the hospital after a misadventure. Once she got her head stuck in a bucket and had to be rescued by a fireman (she said she was trying to find out what her voice sounded like inside the bucket).

In 1957 the family moved to the subsidized housing project Bronxdale, where a diverse community of immigrants and other minorities lived in relative harmony at that time, providing Sonia with a multicultural experience that probably has contributed to her empathy for people of all backgrounds. She and her brother attended Blessed Sacrament, a nearby Catholic elementary school. Their mother's constant striving for improvement inspired them to work hard in school and to read as much as they could. She often told them, "I don't care what you do, but be the best at it."[5]

Sonia faced her first major obstacle at the age of eight, when she was diagnosed with Type I diabetes. She was told that because of her medical problems she would have to abandon her ambition to become a detective like her fictional hero Nancy Drew, so she turned her sights on the law, inspired by the television series Perry Mason. At that time, it was believed that even with assiduous care, diabetes could shorten one's life by decades. Far from holding her back, her diabetes pushed her to work even harder, pushing ahead throughout her career, trying to accomplish as much as possible in what little time she had. She was very disciplined about watching her diet and controlling her blood sugar, and when she was being vetted for the Supreme Court nomination, Dr. Paul Robertson of the American Diabetes Association stated that she was a good role model for patients struggling with diabetes, and that her example would "go a long way toward being a major push against the stigma

5 Gitlin 21.

that some people with diabetes feel."[6]

A year after her diagnosis, Sonia faced another setback when her father died of a heart attack. Besides the emotional toll, the family had to move into a smaller apartment in the same complex, and their budget became even more restricted. Celina worked long hours as a nurse and Sonia sometimes had to stay with her aunt, who worked in a clandestine sweatshop, where Sonia was not allowed to approach the door to seek relief from the suffocating heat. Regardless of all the limitations, almost every summer the family managed to visit their relatives in Puerto Rico, where Sonia's Latina soul was nourished and she found joy in the family gatherings and the beautiful beaches.

During her last year at Blessed Sacrament, Sonia joined a group of students who got together after school to listen to popular songs and analyze lyrics. Charles Auffant, the group's organizer, told of an incident one afternoon when they were discussing "Sgt. Pepper's Lonely Hearts Club Band." Several of the students offered what they considered to be deep philosophical interpretations, but Sonia said, "You know, we really can't tell what that song means. We need more facts."[7] According to Auffant, that remark drained all the fun out of the conversation, but in retrospect, Sonia's statement was a rather humorous precursor of her present-day attitude toward the law.

Sonia graduated at the top of her class and went on to Cardinal Spellman High School, where she was active on the debate team and in the Latino organization ASPIRA, and she had a boyfriend, Kevin Noonan. In spite of having to move to a new project in the

---

6 Felix 213.
7 Coplon 1/1. Numbers after articles found online indicate the page number on the print-out/total number of pages, as a general indication of where to find the information in the article. See Works Cited for complete information.

north Bronx called Co-op City and having to work part time at a hospital, Sonia graduated with the highest GPA and won a speech contest that entitled her to deliver the valedictory address at graduation.

### Princeton and Yale: S.S. de Noonan, Champion of causes not yet won

Sonia earned admission and a scholarship to Princeton University, even though her SAT scores, according to her, were probably lower than those of some of her classmates. She describes herself as a poster child for Affirmative Action and takes pride in being proof of the benefits of this program. However, she has spoken out about the bias in tests used for admissions and promotions, so her feelings about this issue are complex and will be addressed again later in this chapter. At Princeton, she quickly realized that she had some catching up to do, in spite of having worked so hard at the Catholic schools she attended. Most of her classmates had attended more expensive private schools and thus had the advantage of a more rigorous preparation for college, so she sought the help of several dedicated professors in order to improve her writing and analytical abilities. She found friendship and support in the student organization *Acción Puertorriqueña* and in the Third World Center, an activities facility for minorities. She worked in the school cafeteria and participated in a work-study program to recruit more Latino students, and most importantly, she confirmed her identity as a confident *Nuyorican*, or New York Puerto Rican. In response to a group complaint that she organized, the university created a new class on Puerto Rican history and politics, and increased efforts to recruit Latino faculty and administrators.

At Princeton, Sonia had her first experience with community

service. She organized a volunteer program for Latino students to spend time with Hispanic patients at Trenton Psychiatric Hospital who had been isolated by their inability to speak English. The students served as translators and organized cultural events and holiday celebrations for the patients. This work helped Sonia realize that she would get her greatest professional satisfaction from public service.

At Princeton, Sonia was accepted in the honor society Phi Beta Kappa, awarded the highest honor given to Princeton undergraduates (the Taylor Pyne Prize), and graduated *summa cum laude*. Shortly after graduation, she married her high school sweetheart, Kevin Noonan, and changed her name to Sonia Sotomayor de Noonan, following the Spanish tradition. Her classmates gave her a nickname that reveals something about her character -"S.S. de Noonan"- because even as an undergraduate she was as formidable as an ocean vessel.[8] More light is shed on Sonia's character by the Princeton yearbook of that year, which quotes her as saying, "I am not the champion of lost causes, I am the champion of causes not yet won."[9]

Sonia worked her way through Yale law school with a combination of scholarships and various jobs, while her husband was working on his Ph.D. She was an editor of the *Yale Law Journal* and managing editor of *Yale Studies in World Public Order*. One of her former classmates described her as intellectually tough, willing to stand up for herself, and not intimidated by anybody.[10] During her last year at law school, she was offended by racist questions that were put to her in a job interview by a partner in the firm Shaw, Pitman, Potts & Trowbridge. She was asked, for example, "Do law firms do a disservice by hiring minority students who the firms know do not have the necessary credentials and will then fire

8 Felix 56.
9 David (video).
10 "Judge Sonia Sotomayor" 1/3.

in three to four years?"[11] In spite of the obvious risk to her career, she lodged a formal complaint against this powerful firm, which resulted in a lukewarm written apology from the firm. Not satisfied with this result, Sonia organized a group protest and received support from significant numbers of faculty and students. When threatened with the possibility of being banned from recruiting on the Yale campus, the partners of the firm delivered a much more meaningful apology. This incident increased awareness of racial discrimination on campus and called attention to the problem of biased questions used during the interviewing process.

### Assistant District Attorney: Convicting the Tarzan Burglar

Due to a chance meeting with New York District Attorney Robert Morgenthau during her last term at Yale, Sonia got a job as Assistant DA in Manhattan right after graduation, a position she held from 1979 to 1984. Morgenthau created an atmosphere of thoughtfulness and idealism in his office, and instilled in his assistants a set of practical ethical standards and work habits that would influence the rest of their careers. During the confirmation hearings for the Supreme Court, Morgenthau remembered Sonia as an "able champion of the law" who would be "highly qualified for any position in which wisdom, intelligence, collegiality and good character could be assets."[12] At Yale, Sonia learned critical analysis as well as legal theory, and participated in mock trials, but while working at the DA's office she learned to consider real-world facts and situations and to make arguments based on the laws as they applied to those facts. Although putting people behind bars might not appear to be an idealistic profession, Sonia explained her motivation by pointing out that minorities are the most frequent and vulnerable victims of crime, and she was prosecuting

---

11 Felix 62.
12 Morgenthau 1/1.

the criminals that victimized them. Crime rates were soaring in New York, and the sheer volume of work and stress contributed to Sonia's becoming a chain smoker and a caffeine addict. She had to inject herself with insulin several times a day, which she sometimes did in a colleague's office, and sometimes in the middle of a meeting without missing a beat. She won convictions in a high-profile child porn case and in the Tarzan Burglar case, which involved multiple murders committed by an acrobatic criminal who swung from adjacent buildings to enter windows of his victims' apartments. For the latter case, she accompanied detectives into dangerous neighborhoods full of drug dealers and addicts in order to see the crime scenes in person. Her long hours away from home, usually from 7:00 a.m. to 10:00 p.m., may have contributed to the deterioration of her marriage, which ended in divorce in 1983. A few years later, while participating in a discussion of women in the workplace, Sonia mentioned that her heavy workload was a "contributing factor" in their decision to separate.[13] Kevin had completed his Ph.D. and was planning to go to law school in Chicago, so they were on separate paths. Sonia went back to using her maiden name.

## Private practice: Chasing down fake Guccis

True to her ambition to continue moving up quickly in her profession, Sonia left the DA's office after five years and accepted a position at the private firm Pavia and Harcourt, partly because she wanted to get more experience with international law. At this firm, where she eventually became a partner, she was a general civil litigator involved in commercial law regarding real estate, banking, and contracts, and her clients were often international companies. While working at this firm she participated on the New York Anti-

---

13 "Women in the Workplace." Replayed on "Sonia Sotomayor: Then and Now."

counterfeiting Task Force, created to combat the production of fake namebrand items with labels such as Gucci, Fendi, or Rolex, which often were produced in sweatshops by child labor. Sonia and her colleague Heather McDonald sometimes accompanied security teams on their raids of counterfeiting businesses in Chinatown or Harlem. Rather than following protocol by waiting in a van, they would strap on bulletproof vests and rush into shops with the security officers. Sonia's former coworker Steven Skulnik described one such raid: "I was crouched in the van, waiting for things to clear up, and Sonia goes running out with the investigators. She got a thrill out of the cops and robbers stuff. It's not something you expect to see from a corporate attorney."[14]

All the while excelling at her demanding career, Sonia continued to be generous and helpful to her family and friends, and to donate significant time to community organizations. She worked pro bono on the boards of several civil rights groups, including the Puerto Rican Legal Defense and Education Fund, which advocates for the rights of Puerto Ricans and encourages Latinos to enter the legal profession.

### Federal judge: Saving baseball

In November of 1991, Senator Daniel Patrick Moynihan recommended to President George H.W. Bush that he nominate Sonia to the U.S. District Court for the Southern District of New York, which included Manhattan, the Bronx, and six counties north of New York City. Almost a year later, at the age of 38, she was confirmed by the Senate Judiciary Committee and became the youngest member of the federal court, and the first Latino judge on the federal court in New York. One of the duties of this job that she enjoyed the most was swearing in new citizens, because she

---

14 Sloan 1/1.

was pleased to be helping immigrants take this important step.

As a federal judge, Sonia soon gained a reputation as a defender of the freedoms protected by the Bill of Rights, including freedom of the press, freedom of assembly, and freedom of expression. She upheld the freedom of the press when she ruled that the suicide note of Vincent Foster, a White House Counsel, should be released to the Wall Street Journal. She reaffirmed freedom of assembly when she decided that the Hells Angels should be allowed to stay in their building because there was insufficient evidence of drug dealing. Freedom of expression was affirmed when Sonia reversed a law in White Plains, New York, that banned the public showing of religious or political symbols in city parks.[15] She also defended the rights of the homeless when she ruled that they should be paid appropriately for their work for two nonprofit organizations who claimed their work was "job training," and only paid them $1.00 an hour.[16]

Sonia heard approximately 450 cases between 1992 and 1998. One of her most famous cases occurred in 1995, when she ruled against Major League Baseball owners, ending a baseball strike that had caused the cancellation of the World Series the previous year.[17] She was widely praised for protecting labor laws and saving baseball from another lost season, something which the baseball commissioners, Congress, and the U.S. President all had tried and failed to do. Years later, shortly after beginning her work on the Supreme Court, the New York Yankees showed their appreciation when they invited her to throw the first ceremonial pitch at the September 26, 2009 game against the Red Sox at Yankee Stadium in the Bronx. The photos and video that show her throwing that pitch reveal a woman who is overwhelmed with gratitude and disbelief at her own good fortune. Obviously, her heart remains

15 Gitlin 48-49.
16 Felix 160-161.
17 "Judge Sonia Sotomayor" 2/3.

connected to the Bronx in spite of her incredible success.

## Appellate judge: Overcoming stereotypes

In 1997 President Clinton nominated Sonia to the Second Circuit Court of Appeals, the second most powerful court in the land. Having impeccable credentials and a record of impartial and fair decisions, being registered as an Independent voter, and having been nominated by a Republican president to the District Court, the confirmation process should have gone smoothly for Sonia. However, there were many delays due to partisan politics, and the Republicans' questioning of her was particularly harsh, perhaps because they feared that the next step for her would be a nomination to the Supreme Court. Latino groups throughout the nation wrote thousands of letters to pressure the Senate to confirm her nomination, and she was finally confirmed as a Judge to the Second Circuit Court of Appeals in October of 1998. The grueling process had taken its toll, and Sonia remarked, "Although we all wish to believe that appointments are only the product of merit, the harsh reality is that the support of community groups is critical to insuring that meritorious candidates are not overlooked or victimized in the appointment process...stereotyping is perhaps the most insidious of all problems in our society today."[18]

At the swearing-in ceremony, Sonia thanked her fiancé for making her a better, more loving, and more generous person. She was referring to Peter White, a New York contractor whom she met in 1994. It's possible that this relationship, like her previous marriage, fell victim to Sonia's relentless work load, since the couple separated less than two years later.[19] "There is a price to pay in terms of your personal life," Sonia had commented back in

18 Smith 1/1.
19 Greene 129.

1986,[20] and she continues to pay it.

Many of Sonia's clerks have commented about the amount of detail she would require from lower court rulings. She would study every angle of each case and "work it to death" until she was satisfied that she was ready to rule. During the eleven years that she served on the Second Circuit, Sonia made 3000 panel decisions and wrote approximately 400 published opinions. According to a White House press release, "She works tirelessly to probe both the factual details and the legal doctrines in the cases before her and to arrive at decisions that are faithful to both. She understands that upholding the rule of law means going beyond legal theory to ensure consistent, fair, common-sense application of the law to real-world facts."[21] One of the cases that Sonia considered particularly important was *Ford vs. McGinnis*, in which she reversed a lower court's decision and thus protected an inmate's First Amendment right to celebrate a holiday feast that was important to his practice of Islam.[22] Moreover, she made a ruling that revoked the U.S. citizenship of a man charged with working for the Nazis during World War II, and ordered further consideration of the asylum claims of spouses and boyfriends of Chinese women who had been victims of forced abortion.[23]

While serving as an appellate judge, Sonia taught courses and conducted workshops at six different universities, including New York University and Columbia Law School. She also found time to give more than 80 speeches, in which she expressed both her enthusiasm for the law and her interest in inspiring women and minorities to enter the profession. During this time she served on a selection committee for college scholarships and on the Second Circuit Task Force on Gender, Racial and Ethnic Fairness in the

20 "Women in the Workplace."
21 "Judge Sonia Sotomayor" 2/3.
22 Felix 199.
23 "Judge Sonia Sotomayor" 2/3.

Courts. She was very active on several public boards, including the State of New York Mortgage Agency, which helped low-income people obtain low-rate mortgages; the New York City board to manage campaign spending, for which she insisted on the highest standards; and the board of the Maternity Center, on which she strove to improve maternity care. She dedicated as many as eight hours a week to these pro bono activities –the equivalent of an extra day's work– while remaining committed to her family, co-workers, and community. Besides maintaining regular contact with her mother, she has been devoted to her brother Juan's three children and to her many other godchildren. She made an effort to greet and get to know all of her assistants at work. Her community service has included mentoring young students from troubled neighborhoods and conducting workshops for the Development School for Youth program.[24]

## The Supreme nomination: Murder boards and media mania

On her way to the gym in late April 2009, Sonia received a phone call that would set an historic process in motion. It was a member of President Obama's staff, calling to ask her to contact the White House Legal Counsel Office. When Sonia called, she was informed that the President wanted to include her on his list of candidates to replace Justice David Souter, who was retiring from the Supreme Court. Subsequently, Sonia went through an extensive background check, including interviews with her doctor, Andrew Jay Drexler, about her overall health and control of her diabetes. Dr. Drexler provided a letter to the White House in which he declared that Sonia was in very good health and that she had maintained excellent control over her blood sugar in the two decades that he had supervised her healthcare.[25] As mentioned

---

24 Ibid. 3/3.
25 Stolberg 1/2.

above, Dr. Paul Robertson of the American Diabetes Association also declared that she was a good role model for people diagnosed with diabetes. The President's list of candidates consisted of Sonia plus three other women: Elena Kagan (then Solicitor General, now Associate Justice on the Supreme Court after being confirmed on August 5, 2010); Janet Napolitano, Secretary of Homeland Security; and Diane Wood of the Seventh Circuit Court of Appeals. Sonia was the only one that President Obama did not know personally.

When she finally had the opportunity to meet the president, at the end of a long day of interviews, she almost fainted. It was a momentous occasion, the meeting of the first black president and potentially the first Hispanic Supreme Court justice, both "offspring of the civil rights era" whose intellectual abilities and steadfast resolution had led them down extraordinarily successful paths. This encounter has even more resonance if one considers the interesting parallels between Sonia and the president's intelligent and charismatic wife. Michelle Obama was born ten years after Sonia, grew up in a working-class neighborhood and attended Chicago public schools, then went on to Princeton and ultimately Harvard Law School. She was working at a Chicago law firm, Sidley & Austin, when she met her husband. Although her legal career has been put on hold, Michelle has inspired many people with her courage, strength, and grace under fire. Moreover, she has participated in the advancement of several causes, including poverty awareness and the promotion of healthy eating and exercise in order to combat childhood obesity.[26]

Twelve years earlier, when Sonia was nominated to the Court of Appeals, there was talk that the position could lead to a place for her on the Supreme Court. Subsequently, she was on President Clinton's short list, but no opening became available. Shortly after the historic election of 2008, Latino leaders began a concerted effort to get Sonia nominated to the highest court. After some

26 "First Lady Michelle Obama."

debate, both the Congressional Hispanic Caucus and the Black Caucus agreed to support Sonia's candidacy. Thus, these two major groups, encompassing a wide variety of backgrounds and interests, managed to put aside their differences and rivalries in order to give significant support to the most viable candidate. When the President finally called to offer Sonia the nomination at 8:10 p.m. on May 25, she walked over to the balcony of her apartment with her phone in her left hand and her other hand over her chest, trying to slow down her pounding heart. She caught her breath, started to cry, but managed to murmur, "Thank you, Mr. President." Then, she said, the President asked her to make him two promises: "The first was to remain the person I was, and the second was to stay connected to my community. I said to him that those were two easy promises to make, because those two things I could not change."[27] Sonia asked a friend to drive her to Washington, where her family was already waiting for her. Driving in a blinding rainstorm with a dysfunctional GPS, they got lost on the way and had to call a friend for directions, finally arriving in Washington at 2:30 on the morning of the announcement.[28]

At a press conference later that day, President Obama made the anticipated announcement, praising Sonia for having overcome barriers and having accomplished so much while always remembering where she began and keeping close contact with her community. "What Sonia will bring to the Court, then," he emphasized, "is not only the knowledge and experience acquired over a course of a brilliant legal career, but the wisdom accumulated from an inspiring life's journey."[29] A White House aide had placed Sonia's written response on the podium for her, with the pages accidentally scrambled. Thus, Sonia spoke from memory, and from her heart. She began by expressing her deep

---

27 Swain.

28 Ibid.

29 Felix 218.

gratitude to her friends and family members who had gathered in Washington for the announcement, particularly her brother Juan, who is now a physician in Syracuse, New York, and then made special mention of Celina Sotomayor: "My mother has devoted her life to my brother and me.... I have often said that I am all I am because of her, and I am only half the woman she is." Then she described her commitment to her profession: "I chose to be a lawyer and ultimately a judge because I find endless challenge in the complexities of the law. I firmly believe in the rule of law as the foundation for all of our basic rights." She described a private tour that she was given of the White House eleven years earlier during the confirmation process for her Circuit Court appointment, and commented, "Yet never in my wildest childhood imaginings did I ever envision that moment, let alone did I ever dream that I would live this moment."[30]

Later, in a speech at a reception for her, Obama explained, "[Her appointment] is about every child who will grow up thinking to him or herself, if Sonia Sotomayor can make it, then maybe I can, too.... It's about everyone in this nation facing challenges and struggles in their lives, who hears Justice Sotomayor's story and thinks, if she could overcome so much and go so far, then why can't I?"[31] In a White House press release, it was made clear why Sonia was chosen as the most qualified candidate. She was described as "one of the ablest federal judges currently sitting" and "a role model of aspiration, discipline, commitment, intellectual prowess and integrity." Furthermore, according to this release, "If confirmed, Sonia would bring more federal judicial experience to the Supreme Court than any justice in 100 years, and more overall judicial experience than anyone confirmed for the Court in the past 70 years." The release also cited her "keen awareness of the law's

---

30 "Full Text: Judge Sonia Sotomayor's Speech." All quotes from this speech can be found here.
31 Felix 218.

impact on everyday life" as well as her "consistent, fair, common-sense application of the law to real-world facts."[32]

Before the Senate confirmation hearings even began, Sonia was tried in the court of public opinion. She endured what was described as an "epithet chorus": among other things, she was called racist, reverse racist, anti-white, radical, a member of the Latino KKK, and a judicial activist out of the mainstream.[33] Anonymous sources were quoted as saying that she was aggressive on the bench, a bully, and not very smart. None of these accusations were supported by her judicial record, and her calm, composed demeanor and intelligent responses throughout the exhausting confirmation process belied the anonymous slurs. Besides the media storm, Sonia endured weeks of "murder boards," during which the White House staff grilled her on recent legal developments, coached her on how to behave during the hearings ("never interrupt a senator"), and stipulated every detail of her wardrobe, even her nail polish. In June, an unfortunate fall as she was rushing through LaGuardia International Airport resulted in a fractured ankle, so she had to hobble through weeks of meetings with 89 senators, many of whom signed her plaster cast. During the hearings, which took place from July 13 – 16, 2009, she was wearing a "walking boot," and she had to elevate her leg on a makeshift footrest that was held together with duct tape.

One of the biggest stumbling blocks to her confirmation was a quote taken out of context from a speech that she had given at the Berkeley La Raza Law Journal's Twelfth Annual Symposium on October 6, 2001. The purpose of her talk was to motivate Latinos to enter the law profession and to describe both the benefits and the responsibilities inherent in being Latino. "My family showed me by their example," she said, "how wonderful and vibrant life is

32 "Judge Sonia Sotomayor" 1/3. All quotes from press release in this paragraph can be found here.
33 Coplon 1/1.

32

and how wonderful and magical it is to have a Latina soul." With a sense of urgency, she quoted statistics that reveal the lack of Latino judges at all levels and observed, "These figures demonstrate that there is a real and continuing need for Latino and Latina organizations and community groups throughout the country to exist and to continue their efforts of promoting women and men of all colors in their pursuit for equality in the judicial system." The controversial words in this speech were: "I would hope that a wise Latina woman with the richness of her experience would more often than not reach a better conclusion than a white male who hasn't lived that life."[34] Senator Jeff Sessions and several other senators interrogated her repeatedly about this statement, even though she had called the quote an unfortunate choice of words, and then explained herself clearly: "My personal and professional experiences help me listen and understand, with the law always commanding the result in every case," she declared, and she stated several times that she would apply the law, not make laws.[35] This declaration is well substantiated by her judicial record.

Jeff Sessions insisted that he believed that her background would play a role in deciding cases, and other conservatives expressed concern that she would make rulings based on personal or political beliefs rather than solely on interpretation of the law itself. Conservatives also questioned her intellectual ability, accusing her of being chosen because of her gender and ethnicity, not for being the best qualified, and implying that her entire career was a product of Affirmative Action rather than her abilities. In spite of these politically motivated attacks and repeated interruptions by antiabortion protesters -who had to be forcefully removed during the hearings- Sonia maintained her composed demeanor and continued to speak calmly at all times, even when some senators

---

34 "Supreme Court Nominee Sonia Sotomayor's Speech at Berkeley Law in 2001."
35 "Text: Sotomayor's opening statement." cbsnews.com.

spoke to her in unusually loud, aggressive tones.

After extensive interrogation that was described as "grueling, repetitive and at times offensive," Sonia was finally confirmed by the senate with a vote of 68-31, "breaking another barrier," according to President Obama, "and moving us yet another step closer to a more perfect union." [36] At the age of 55, Sonia became the 111th Associate Justice of the Supreme Court, the third woman and first Latino to ever be a member of the nation's highest court.

## Supreme Court Justice: strong liberal voice, assertive dissents, and first pitches

During her first day on the Supreme Court, September 9, 2009, Sonia heard oral arguments for the infamous *Citizens United* case, which established the personhood of corporations and their right to inject money into political campaigns. As proof of her intense work ethic, in the one month since her confirmation she had read over 2000 pages of legal briefs for this case, prepared for several other pending cases, moved to Washington D.C., set up her office, and hired four law clerks. She participated actively in the questioning phase, and when the majority decided to overrule two precedents and affirm the First Amendment rights of corporations, Sonia joined three other justices in the dissent. [37] As other cases came before the court, Sonia continued to play a very active role, asking 146 questions by the end of December 2009, as compared to 110 questions asked by Chief Justice Roberts. [38] In spite of some minor gaffes, such as forgetting to turn on her microphone or interrupting a lawyer who was answering a question, she soon became recognized as a forceful representative of liberal causes

---

36 Felix 234.
37 Ibid. 249.
38 Gitlin 90.

who was not afraid to express her opinion in court and during numerous public appearances. Utilizing court recesses to speak with students around the country, Sonia has encouraged them to overcome their self-doubt by confessing her own insecurity: "Almost everything I've done I've been frightened about, including being a Supreme Court justice," she told a large group of students at the University of Chicago Law School in January 2011.[39] During this same talk, she criticized Chief Justice John Roberts' approach to racial equality. Regarding the use of race to achieve public school integration, Roberts wrote in a 2007 opinion that "the way to stop discrimination on the basis of race is to stop discriminating on the basis of race." Sonia remarked that this approach was "too simple." "Our society is too complex to use that kind of analysis," she explained.[40] She also questioned Justice Antonin Scalia's reliance on determining the original meaning of the Constitution. She prefers to consider legislative history when trying to interpret ambiguous statutes, a practice that Scalia avoids.[41]

By June of 2011, Sonia was being hailed as "the most well-known and effective member of the Court's liberal wing."[42] In contrast to other past and present justices who have presented their opinions in technical and academic terms, Sonia has charmed the public by presenting opinions in a format that the general population can understand, as well as making notable public appearances such as throwing the first ceremonial pitch at both Yankee Stadium and Wrigley Field, while wearing the home team's jersey in each case.[43] She has spoken to students at a wide range of venues -including at several law schools, a community college in the Bronx, a bilingual elementary school in Berkeley, and a number of university commencement ceremonies- as well as to members

39 Stohr 1/3.
40 Liptak. 31 Jan 2011, 1/3.
41 Ibid. 2/3.
42 Fontana 1/3.
43 Ibid. 2/3.

of the Juvenile Diabetes Research Foundation. Furthermore, she has received visits at the Supreme Court from representatives of many different groups, including special-needs children, senior citizens and veterans.[44]

Sonia has made numerous remarks about how women, minorities, and low-income people suffer inequalities in the judicial system because of prejudices based on stereotypes. She criticized the blatant gender and ethnic bias that she faced during her confirmation hearings, and she has denounced the persistent "structural problems" that have created barriers to full equality for all people.[45]

In her first terms on the Court, Sonia has concurred with the majority on historic decisions regarding immigration and health care, privacy rights, defendants' rights, and the Fair Sentencing Act. In 2009, according to news anchor Jorge Ramos, she set an example during the case of *Mohawk Industries v. Carpenter* by using the term "undocumented immigrant", in place of the offensive designation of "illegal alien."[46] She also wrote several strong dissents; for example, in a case of what she considered unwarranted immunity for police officers who raided a 73-year-old woman's home in Los Angeles, she criticized the court for limiting the constitutional protection against unreasonable searches.[47] She expressed the lone dissent when the Supreme Court denied a petition to require courts to examine suggestive eyewitness evidence with extra care, a decision which Sonia claimed could undermine the fairness of a trial.[48] In 2011, Sonia dissented when the majority upheld parts of the Arizona immigration law, stating, "The Arizona law runs contrary to the uniformity and expertise

44 Ibid. 2/3.
45 Ibid. 3/3.
46 Ramos 124.
47 "Editorial; Unwarranted Immunity." 1/1.
48 Liptak 1/2. 12 Jan 2012.

in enforcement of immigration law that Congress intended by allowing only federal officials to prosecute and rule upon civil and criminal cases."[49] Subsequently, important parts of this Arizona law were overturned by a June 2012 Supreme Court decision with which Sotomayor concurred. Many provisions of the law were struck down, although the significant "papers please" clause, which allows state police to request immigration papers from anyone detained, was left intact for future deliberation.[50] In an interview with Diane Sawyer, Jorge Ramos objected to the preservation of the "papers please" clause. He was particularly disappointed with Sonia's vote in this case, according to a comment on his website, and during the interview he called this decision "a sad day for the Hispanic community."[51] In this case, it seems that Sonia followed her normal procedure and voted according to the legal arguments presented rather than her personal opinion. She said that she was confused by the government's arguments, which did not mention racial profiling and focused on the federal government's supremacy over state government in this matter.[52] Therefore, she agreed that the case should be left open for further consideration after more information is gathered.

A significant decision with which Sonia concurred was the ruling on June 28, 2012, that the Affordable Care Act is constitutional, a decision that gave a major victory to President Obama.[53] This sweeping reform was designed to improve access to medical services for millions of people, since it dramatically increases the number of people eligible for Medicaid, establishes health insurance exchanges, and prohibits health insurers from denying coverage due to pre-existing conditions.

---

49 "Sonia Sotomayor on Immigration." 1/1.
50 Sacks 1/2.
51 Sawyer (video).
52 Goodwin 1.
53 Ibid. 1.

When people ask Sonia what she wants her legacy to be, she usually replies that she cannot determine that in advance because she prefers to remain open to learning more from each case and from each person she meets. "My highest aspiration for my work on the Court is to grow in understanding beyond what I can foresee, beyond any borders visible from this vantage," she writes. "To remain open to understandings –perhaps even to principles— as yet not determined is the least that learning requires, its barest threshold."[54]

## Advice from a wise Latina

At the 2012 commencement ceremony for NYU, Sonia told the graduating students how they, too, could achieve great things. First, one must overcome one's fears. She confessed that she was afraid of every new thing that she has tried and even felt "absolute fear" at becoming a Supreme Court Justice, but she had to push through her fear and do it anyway. Then, she advised them to remember five essentials: humility, excitement, challenge, gratitude and engagement: humility, to recognize all those who come before you; excitement about learning new things; accepting the challenge to work at bettering the world in every way you can; gratitude to all those who have helped you, since nobody succeeds alone; engagement with your community, and "an incessant optimism that compels you to give to others." She offered this advice not as a roadmap, but as an attitude toward life. "The key to success," she declared, "is continuously maintaining an ever-present curiosity and openness to the joy in learning new things."[55]

In an interview shortly after Sonia began her tenure on the Supreme Court, Susan Swain asked her what she would say to

54 Sotomayor 299 and 301.
55 "Justice Sotomayor's Speech."

young people interested in a career in law. Sonia replied that everyone should pick a career that gives them some joy on a daily basis. She explained that if you like thinking about the problems people are having, reading about ways to solve those problems, and meeting with them in a courtroom to try to sort things out, then you might like to be a lawyer. "The law will let you be a part of everyone's lives, because the law affects every part of our society. We help solve their problems – that to me is the fascination of law," she concluded.[56]

In her interactions with students, Sonia often encourages them to take chances and to risk failure. "Success is its own reward," she comments in her memoir, "but failure is a great teacher too, and not to be feared."[57] When she feels at a disadvantage, Sonia's reaction is to dig in with even greater determination. She learned from her mother's example that "a surplus of effort could overcome a deficit of confidence."[58]

### Her path to success

Sonia has been described as a role model for youthful idealists striving to make a difference in the world, a "bright beacon for those who will someday follow in her footsteps,"[59] and outstanding proof that anything is possible. She takes seriously her responsibility as a role model for young Latinas, and she makes it a high priority to receive visits from Latino groups at the Supreme Court. She has been identified by Latinos as *nuestra héroe* (our hero) because of her hard work, dedication, and commitment to the Latino community. She has shown repeatedly that she has never forgotten her roots, since for Sonia, her history and heritage

56 Swain.
57 Sotomayor 132.
58 Ibid. 115.
59 Greene 172.

are essential to her life and success and "to leave those behind would mean leaving her soul and identity behind as well."[60]

She has overcome many obstacles to success, starting with being raised in a poor neighborhood in the Bronx. Although she insists her childhood was not so difficult, she did have to work summers and take part-time jobs during the academic year throughout her high school and university education. Her odd jobs included working at a clothing store, a bakery, and a bar where she alternated as bouncer and bartender. At Princeton she discovered that her preparation was not comparable to that of her classmates, so she had to scramble to catch up. Her father's death when she was only nine dealt her family a huge blow, resulting in their having to move into a smaller apartment and her mother having to work even harder to make ends meet. Sonia has had to deal with Type I diabetes since she was eight years old, and she has been extremely disciplined about watching her diet and getting exercise, as is required in order to avoid complications. Even so, she did pass out a few times and would have died if someone hadn't intervened in time. Nevertheless, a friend of hers has explained that Sonia takes all the prudent precautions, but "not in a way that makes her a victim of a disease or a person whose life is ruled by a disease."[61] Thus, she has proven to be a vital role model and inspiration for other people with the same diagnosis.

Another obstacle to overcome has been the racial discrimination and gender bias that Sonia has experienced throughout her career. During her last term at Yale, she faced offensive, racist questions during a job interview. Early in her career as a judge, she was sometimes lectured to by older lawyers, who would never think of being so disrespectful to a male judge. As recently as 2009, during her confirmation hearings, conservative senators felt free to question her intellectual capabilities and to express doubts that

60 Ibid. 172.
61 Stolberg 2/2.

she could make rulings without showing favor to certain groups.

This brings us back to the important question of Sonia's feelings about being a poster child for Affirmative Action. Publicly, she has chosen to interpret this in a positive way, showing pride in being able to provide proof that the program works, but in private she must feel some resentment at the implication that she only succeeded because she received preferential treatment based on her gender and ethnicity. She addressed this issue directly when she lodged a complaint against the law firm whose partner insulted her during a recruitment interview. In her memoir, she wrote: "I had no need to apologize that the look-wider, search-more affirmative action that Princeton and Yale practiced had opened doors for me. That was its purpose: to create the conditions whereby students from disadvantaged backgrounds could be brought to the starting line of a race many were unaware was even being run."[62] She points out that Affirmative Action only opens doors, and then students have to work extremely hard to catch up to their classmates, graduate, and succeed in their careers.

Sonia has made it past all of these roadblocks, but along the way there have been some tolls to pay. After her nomination to the Supreme Court, she lamented her loss of privacy and calm. There have been days she wished her life were a little quieter, and she admits that she misses being able to walk the streets unnoticed. Her personal life has been affected, as is common in the legal profession. In 2009, 50% of female lawyers were unmarried, compared to 15% of male lawyers.[63] Sonia's intense commitment to work and her long hours probably contributed to her divorce and, years later, to the separation from her second fiancé. During her first term on the Supreme Court, Sonia made this wry observation: "I understand from my girlfriends that I've been put on a most-eligible bachelorette list, but right now I pity the man who tries

62 Sotomayor 191.
63 Felix 202.

to find a minute in my schedule."[64] Another price she has paid is not having children of her own. Although Sonia has found great joy in being an aunt and a godmother to numerous children, she sometimes regrets not being a mother.

So how has Sonia overcome these obstacles, and dealt with the burdens she has had to bear? Sonia often downplays the difficulties she encountered along her path to success, and she makes no claim to being exceptional. During her speech at the announcement of her nomination to the Supreme Court, Sonia declared, "I am an ordinary person who has been blessed with extraordinary opportunities and experiences,"[65] thus giving credit to other people and external circumstances. Undoubtedly, there are elements of her own character that have contributed to her success as well.

Her family has supported her in many ways. Her father believed that the United States was a land of opportunity and that his children could do whatever they dreamed of doing. He told Sonia that some day she would go to the moon (perhaps she has, in a figurative sense). Sonia's mother propelled her along her path with words, telling her to do the best she could at whatever she did; with actions, serving as an example by working overtime and studying side-by-side at the kitchen table with her children; and with her investment of hard-earned money in private schools and an expensive set of encyclopedias, thus making education a high priority in the family. Sonia had to protect her younger brother Juan from neighborhood bullies, and her instinct to defend him probably contributed to her becoming "tough as nails," as Juan has described her.[66] Her extended family, especially her *Abuelita*, fed her Latina soul and provided a context in which she could feel the security of family traditions, gain confidence, and rejoice in

64 Saltonstall 1/1.
65 "Full Text: Judge Sonia Sotomayor's Speech." 3/3.
66 Felix 25.

music, dancing and laughter.

Besides her family, friends, and mentors, there were certain circumstances that favored Sonia's progress. Her diagnosis of diabetes at the age of eight was a terrible blow that she was told would cut short her life and make it impossible for her to follow her dream of being a detective. However, as proof that what happens to you can be less important than how you react to it, there were significant improvements in Sonia's life as a result of this diagnosis. Medical attention changed her from a tired, listless child who was not interested in school to a dedicated and energetic student, eager to take on new challenges. She switched her goal of becoming a detective to pursuing a career in law. This was a significant change, since it is hard to imagine her achieving national recognition as a private investigator. Besides motivating her to achieve as much as possible in what little time she had, the diagnosis also contributed to her becoming extremely disciplined at a young age, which probably helped her with her studies, her workload, and her overall health.

Sonia was able to take advantage of certain opportunities, such as living in a multicultural neighborhood close to a good private school, receiving scholarships and work-study jobs, receiving extra help from professors, meeting the Manhattan District Attorney by chance, and having her nominations be supported by Latino organizations. Nevertheless, there are elements of Sonia's character that have contributed to her success. She is a fun-loving person who knows how to have a good time: on the night before her investiture at the Supreme Court, she went out dancing at a karaoke bar in Washington D.C. and joined a few of her relatives in a lively rendition of the Sister Sledge song "We are family."[67] That same month she was filmed dancing the salsa with actor Esai Morales at a celebratory bash, while wearing a glittery black outfit

---

67 Ibid. 240.

and pointy-toed stiletto heels.[68] Sonia has a great sense of humor, and of Latina pride. At the White House celebration after her confirmation, she showed off her newly manicured, fire-engine red nail polish to President Obama, who joked that she had been briefed about using neutral colors. Unabashed, Sonia showed off her semi-hoop earrings and said, "Mr. President, you have no idea what you have unleashed."[69]

Although she takes her work seriously, Sonia does not take *herself* seriously. In 2012, she appeared on the children's television show "Sesame Street" and carefully explained to the bouncing puppets exactly what a Supreme Court justice does. She spoke some Spanish with them and then conducted a mock trial of Goldilocks. When all the puppets clamored for help solving their problems, she very patiently listened to the details of their conflicts and offered legal advice.[70]

Sonia is known for her generosity to family, friends, colleagues and staff. For many years she hosted an extravagant Christmas party at the federal courthouse and gave gifts to over sixty co-workers and the entire custodial and lunchroom staff. At one of the parties thrown in her honor after her confirmation to the Supreme Court, she thanked all twenty of the kitchen workers in person and posed with them for a group photograph. The head chef commented, "She showed us —all these Latino immigrants who were in the kitchen working to make the meal special—that she is one of us."[71]

Obviously, Sonia was born with brains. However, she has

---

68 "Supreme Court Justice Sonia Sotomayor Dancing the Salsa in DC."
69 Saxon-Parrish 110.
70 "The Justice Hears a Case."
71 Saxon-Parrish 115.

systematically developed her intellectual prowess by studying intensely throughout her education and career, welcoming any opportunity to learn something new, analyzing every detail of a case until she thoroughly understands all of its complexities, and reading, reading, reading until her brain aches. A brain is a muscle, she says, and she exercises it every day. She learned vital observational skills by listening and watching for hints of an impending storm in her volatile family, and these skills have served her well in the courtroom. She honed her speaking ability by participating on the high school debate team and engaging in lively discussions about everything from politics to song lyrics. She has perfected her writing style by editing law journals and writing hundreds of legal opinions. Moreover, her memoir reveals that before every important interview or confirmation hearing she prepared as if her life depended on it.

Sonia has developed cultural sensitivity and knowledge by making numerous trips to Puerto Rico, studying its language and history, and maintaining her connection to Latino culture in general. She identifies the Spanish language as an important key to understanding her heritage: "Of all the links, language remains strong, a code of the soul that unlocks for us the music and poetry, the history and literature of Spain and all of Latin America."[72] She finds strength and inspiration in her family and community: "There are strengths in our collective psyche that account for our resilience and that equally hold the potential for our renewal, if properly nourished and cultivated. I could see it in my own mother's reverence for education, her faith in community, her infinite capacity for hard work and perserverance; in Abuelita's joyful generosity, her passion for life and poetry, her power to heal. Such strong women are no rarity in our culture."[73]

Sonia's incredible success story is not just about the people

---

72 Sotomayor 157.
73 Ibid. 151.

who have helped her and the opportunities that she has had, but, most importantly, it is about what she has done with those opportunities and how she, in turn, has helped and inspired countless others. Her courageous and joyful spirit, lighthearted sense of humor, generosity toward others, fierce determination, intense intellectual curiosity and willingness to take on new challenges have all contributed to her success. In college, she was the defender of causes yet to be won. Now she is the defender of causes that are being won, incrementally or with dramatic breakthroughs, and she has helped to make that happen.

§ § §

# Works Cited

## Books

Felix, Antonia. *Sonia Sotomayor: The True American Dream*. New York: Berkeley Publishing Group, 2010.

Gitlin, Marty. *Sonia Sotomayor: Supreme Court Justice*. Edina, MN: ABDO Publishing Company, 2011.

Greene, Meg. *Sonia Sotomayor: A Biography*. Santa Barbara: Greenwood Biographies, 2012.

Ramos Avalos, Jorge. *A Country for All: An Immigrant Manifesto*. Trans. Ezra Fitz. New York: Random House, 2010.

Sotomayor, Sonia. *My Beloved World*. New York: Alfred A. Knopf, 2013.

## Articles and web pages (web pages accessed Aug - Sep, 2012)

Coplon, Jeff. "Precedents; Sotomayor's original intent." *New York*. 12 Oct 2009. http://go.galegroup.com.

David, Priya (reporter). "Sonia Sotomayor in Depth." *CBS News*. 26 May 2009. CBSNewsOnline. http://www.youtube.com.

"Editorial; Unwarranted Immunity." *New York Times*. 24 Feb 2012. http://www.nytimes.com.

First Lady Michelle Obama." The White House website. http://

www.whitehouse.gov.

Fontana, David. "Sonia Sotomayor: How She Became the Public Face of the Supreme Court's Liberal Wing." *The New Republic*. 29 Jun 2011. http://www.tnr.com.

"Full Text: Judge Sonia Sotomayor's Speech." *Time*. 26 May 2009. http://www.time.com.

Goodwin, Liz. "Supreme Court upholds key part of Arizona immigration law." *ABC News*. 25 Jun 2012. http://abcnews.go.com.

"Judge Sonia Sotomayor." The White House Office of the Press Secretary. 26 May 2009. http://www.whitehouse.gov.

"Justice Sotomayor's Speech." NYU 2012 commencement. http://www.youtube.com.

"The Justice Hears a Case." http://www.youtube.com.

Liptak, Adam. "Eyewitness Evidence Needs No Special Cautions, Court Says." *New York Times*. 12 Jan 2012. http://www.nytimes.com/2012/01/12 .

---. "Sotomayor Reflects on First Years on Court." *New York Times*. 31 Jan 2011. http://www.nytimes.com/2011/02/01.

Morgenthau, Robert M. "Sotomayor Is Highly Qualified." *Wall Street Journal*. 9 May 2009.

Sacks, Mike. "Arizona Immigration Law Ruling: Supreme Court Delivers Split Decision." *Huffington Post*. 25 Jun 2012. http://www.huffingtonpost.com/2012/06/25 .

Saltonstall, David. "Justice Sonia Sotomayor looking for law not love; still humbled by appointment." *NY Daily News*. 19 Dec 2009. http://www.nydailynews.com/news/2009/12/19 .

Sawyer, Diane. "World News with Diane Sawyer." *ABC News*. 25 Jun 2012. http://www.youtube.com.

Saxon-Parrish, Shani. "Her Honor: A Portrait of Justice Sonia Sotomayor." *Latina*. Dec-Jan 2009. Article based on a story by Sandra Guzmán. http://www.latina.com.

Sloan, Karen. "Nominee's civil practice was with a small, but specialized firm." *Law.com*. 28 May 2009. http://www.law.com.

Smith, Greg B. "Judge's Journey to Top: Bronx' Sotomayor Rose from Projects to Court of Appeals." *New York Daily News*. 24 Oct 1998. 17.

"Sonia Sotomayor on Immigration." *On The Issues*. http://www.ontheissues.org.

"Sonia Sotomayor: Then and Now." *ABC News*. 18 Jun 2009. Replay of 1986 panel "Women in the Workplace."

"Sotomayor's judicial philosophy: 'Fidelity to the law'." *Los Angeles Times*. 14 Jul 2009. http://articles.latimes.com/2009/jul/14.

Stohr, Greg. "Justice Sotomayor Becomes a Forceful Voice as Obama Top Court Appointee." http://www.bloomberg.com.

Stolberg, Sheryl Gay. "Court Nominee Manages Diabetes With Discipline." *New York Times*. 10 Jul 2009. http://www.nytimes.com/2009/07/10.

"Supreme Court case Chamber of Commerce v. Whiting." Cited in "Sonia Sotomayor on Immigration." *On The Issues*. 8 Dec 2010. http.www.ontheissues.org.

"Supreme Court Justice Sonia Sotomayor Dancing Salsa in DC." http://www.youtube.com.

"Supreme Court Nominee Sonia Sotomayor's Speech at Berkeley Law in 2001." 2009 Archive. http://www.law.berkeley.edu.

Swain, Susan. "Interview with Justice Sonia Sotomayor." C-SPAN. 16 Sep 2009. http://www.c-spanvideo.org.

"Tango Sotomayor." *The Vic and Paul Show.* 25 Aug 2010. http://www.youtube.com.

"Text: Sonia Sotomayor's Opening Statement." *Political Hotsheet – CBS News.* 13 Jul 2009. http://www.cbsnews.com.

"The Justice Hears a Case." http://www.youtube.com.

"Women in the Workplace." A panel discussion moderated by Joan Luden.

## Dolores Huerta

(Strike)     At a rally

Explaining the grape boycott.     President Obama awards
Dolores the Medal of Freedom

## Chapter Two

## Dolores Huerta: Union Organizer and Community Activist

"I'll just keep going for as long as I can, and die with my boots on."

--Dolores Huerta (still going at the age of 84)

Tigress, La Pasionaria, the Indomitable Dolores, Seven Tongues, Dragon Lady, the New Mestiza, a non-traditional Chicana, upstart, shoot-from-the-hip woman, formidable adversary, fearless warrior, firebrand, unsung heroine, symbol of justice and fairness. . . a list of nicknames and epithets associated with Dolores Huerta tells a complex tale of rebellion, determination and courageous action. Dolores[74], the co-founder of United Farm Workers (UFW), often appears in public wearing jeans and a cotton T-shirt with a union logo on it, even when she is the invited speaker at a large university. Her natural beauty was described in the year 2000, when she was 70, with these words: "Her bottle-black hair frames a face easily mistaken for 20 or more years younger. Ancestral genes play well on her high cheekbones and on her full lips captured parenthetically by dimples."[75] More than a decade later, she has a few more wrinkles

---

74 I ask Dolores' and the reader's forgiveness for the use of her first name. It is my attempt to get close to my subject, and to help the reader identify with her.

75 Drake 3/3 (3/3 indicates the third page of a three-page print-out from a website.)

and gray hairs, but the description still applies. Her character is as remarkable as her physical appearance: "Unflappable as a union organizer, uncompromising as a contract negotiator, unapologetic as she lived against the grain of the social and political norms of her era, she leaves an indelible legacy of labor-organizing in United States history."[76]

In a modest assessment of her legacy, Dolores gives much of the credit for the success of the UFW to the farmworkers: "César and I were at the helm, but it was the workers who did the work and made the sacrifices and some of them even gave their lives. I was fortunate to have a part in everything we did, but without the workers, nothing would have happened. So I would say that the history of the UFW is not about an individual legacy, but a collective legacy."[77]

Dolores' early activism played out against the backdrop of the progressive movements of the 60s and 70s in this country, including the Chicano Movement, Lyndon Johnson's Great Society programs, and Women's Liberation. As a nontraditional activist, Dolores had a few precursors in the previous generation of Chicana labor organizers, such as Luisa Moreno (1907-1992), Josefina Fierro de Bright (1914-1998) and Emma Tenayucca (1916-1999). However, most of the Latina activists, even in Dolores' generation, worked behind the scenes and in support of their men. César Chávez's wife Helen is an example of the many women who furthered the cause in more traditional ways. In contrast, Dolores was often on the front lines, and she has paid a high price for her fearless advocacy, including having received death threats from her opponents. She has been arrested twenty-four times for participating in nonviolent protests, and she was beaten so badly by a San Francisco police officer that she was hospitalized with five broken ribs and a ruptured spleen. Even after she suffered a

76 Chávez, 240.
77 García, Kay. "Interview with Dolores Huerta."

crippling brain aneurysm that disabled her for many months, she resumed her participation in marches and demonstrations as soon as possible. In spite of her critical role in the success of the UFW, for decades she was perceived as the woman behind César Chávez. However, in more recent years she has emerged from his shadow and has been recognized in her own right.

Dolores was inducted into the Women's Hall of Fame in 1993, and since then she has been given a long list of awards and honors, including nine honorary doctorates, the Eleanor Roosevelt Human Rights Award presented to her by President Clinton in 1998, and the Medal of Freedom conferred upon her by President Obama in 2011. The latter award is the highest honor given to civilians in the United States, and when he presented it to her the President explained, "Without any negotiating experience, Dolores helped lead a worldwide grape boycott that forced growers to agree to some of the country's first farm worker contracts. And ever since, she has fought to give more people a seat at the table. 'Don't wait to be invited,' she says, 'Step in there.'"[78]

The Mexican government recently bestowed upon Dolores its highest honor for a civilian living outside of Mexico, the Ohtli Award, whose name refers to the Nahuatl word meaning "path." The award recognizes Dolores' efforts to "forge a new path" for those who have emigrated from Mexico, and the name of the award pays tribute to the language and culture of the Aztecs.[79] Four elementary schools in California as well as one in Fort Worth, Texas, and a high school in Pueblo, Colorado, have been named after her. She has established the Dolores Huerta Foundation to continue her work, and as of 2013, at the age of 83, she is still lecturing and participating in community organization.

---

78 "Remarks by the President at Presidential Medal of Freedom Ceremony"
79 Mexican embassy website.

Although she can fire up a crowd with her inspiring oratory, Dolores also can be mild-mannered and soft-spoken. The mother of eleven children, she now has fourteen grandchildren and six great-grandchildren. She has expressed feelings of guilt for having focused so much of her energy on improving other people's lives while exposing her own children to a life of poverty and transience. Nevertheless, she is proud of how her children have turned out, and she maintains a healthy sense of humor in regard to her sacrifices. Referring to thrift shop bargains and giveaways, Dolores once quipped, "[At least] all of us have very exotic wardrobes. We get our clothes out of donations."[80]

The multifaceted quality of Dolores' identity is of great significance to the generations of Latinos who may follow her lead. César Chávez, the iconic co-founder of the UFW, was more firmly grounded in a traditional Mexican identity, and he sometimes taunted Dolores by accusing her of not being truly Mexican. However, Dolores has demonstrated her ability to navigate between her Mexican and North American identities without sacrificing her sense of self or of either culture. This flexibility, combined with her willingness to cultivate qualities within herself that were not traditionally considered to be feminine, proved to be very valuable when Dolores was lobbying state and national legislators to support bills that would protect farmworkers. She wrote in a letter to César Chávez, "Being a now (ahem) experienced lobbyist, I am able to speak on a man-to-man basis with other lobbyists."[81]

Whether operating on a man-to-man or a woman-to-man basis, Dolores was equally adept at influencing politicians and negotiating with growers for better labor contracts. Sometimes she would appeal to the growers as a woman, describing the hardships endured by women and children in the fields and making the powerful men feel guilty, or when necessary, she

80 García, Richard. 66.
81 Dolores Huerta Foundation website, no page numbers.

would call upon her inner warrior. Chávez sometimes joked about "unleashing Dolores" on the growers,[82] who called her the "Dragon Lady" because of her ability to "speak with fire" when she was defending the interests of UFW members.[83] Chávez described Dolores as "absolutely fearless, physically and emotionally."[84]

When Dolores was asked whether she thought it was more advantageous to assimilate into North American society or to maintain Mexican traditions, she replied that the two cultures have both positive and negative aspects. The Mexican values of venerating elders, supporting family unity, and rejecting materialism are beneficial to communities, for example, but *machismo* (a particularly virulent form of sexism) is detrimental, according to her, and should be eliminated.[85] As for the pros and cons of mainstream North American society, she has praised the more egalitarian attitude toward women in the U.S., and criticized the treatment of minorities and immigrants.

Dolores' challenge to the polarized categories of male/female and North American/Mexican explains why she has been called a "New Mestiza," a term coined by Gloria Anzaldúa to describe a "woman who lives on the border between tradition and non-tradition, and between the accepted and the non-acceptable."[86] Dolores' lifestyle was offensive to many traditionalists because of her two divorces, her subsequent live-in arrangement with Richard Chávez (César's brother), and her attitude toward parenting, which she believed was secondary to the greater cause of political activism. Dolores often brought some of her children with her to the picket line and other union activities. As she matured and became more familiar with the women's liberation movement, she

---

82 Schiff 328.
83 Chávez, 248.
84 Schiff 297.
85 Oliva 4/5.
86 García, Richard. 59.

began to defend her choices, asserting that part of being a good parent is presenting children with opportunities to work toward the common good. She believed that these early experiences could sharpen her children's sense of social responsibility and give them faith in their ability to make a difference.

## Lessons in diversity

Dolores' own childhood provided her with lessons in helping other people and working with diverse groups. She was born in 1930 in the mining town of Dawson, New Mexico, and given the name Dolores Clara Fernandez. Her father, Juan Fernandez, was a miner who went to work in the fields after he was blacklisted for being a union activist. He began to participate in local politics, and eventually earned a seat in the New Mexico legislature, where he worked for progressive labor legislation. He and Dolores' mother, Alicia St. John Chávez, were divorced when Dolores was five. In 1936, Alicia Chávez took her children to the farmworker community of Stockton, California, where Dolores spent the rest of her youth and early adulthood. Alicia Chávez and her children lived in a neighborhood where Chinese, Latinos, Blacks, Native Americans, Italians and Japanese coexisted.[87] The relatively friendly interaction among these groups provided Dolores with an important lesson in the value of diversity.

While raising five children, Alicia Chávez worked hard at any job she could find: in the fields, in a restaurant, and at a canning factory, where she participated in the cannery workers' strike in 1938. She managed to save enough money to buy a restaurant. Later, when offered the opportunity, she took over a 70-room

87 Since most of this biographical information is widely available on multiple websites and in various articles and books (listed in the Bibliography), I only have footnoted the quotes, and the passages that offer a unique perspective.

hotel, where she often allowed poor families to stay for reduced fees or for free. As an independent, ambitious, and compassionate woman, Alicia Chávez set an example for her children and gave them both freedom and opportunities to explore different paths.

In spite of the low-income area in which they lived, Dolores' upbringing included some of the trappings of the middle class. She was an active member of various school clubs, church organizations, and the Girl Scouts; she performed as a majorette and took dance, piano, and violin lessons. At one point Dolores thought she might like to be a professional flamenco dancer, an ambition that evokes a striking visual image of her spirited character. She could have been a flamboyant dancer wearing a colorful, swirling skirt and rattling castanets in her hands, but instead she chose to march defiantly along the picket lines in a simple shirt and pants, holding a cardboard symbol of the UFW.

There were many ethnic groups represented in the Girl Scouts, and Dolores credits their leader, Kathryn Kemp, with teaching them how to work as a team and providing activities such as camping, which they otherwise would not have experienced. Dolores' integrated neighborhood, school, and scout troop provided her with a positive perspective on diversity, but in high school she was confronted by the cruelty of racism. Dolores tried to create a youth club open to a wide variety of students, but the club was shut down by the police after the department received complaints about racial mixing. It was even more painful for Dolores when she received a C in a course for which she had earned an A, because the teacher thought that someone else had done the work for her. In another unfortunate incident, Dolores was denied a prize that she had won in a school contest to sell the most war bonds. According to her, the contest organizers could not admit that a Mexican American had won the competition.

Dolores took these early lessons to heart. In the summers,

she usually worked in her mother's restaurant, but one year she defied her mother's wishes and went to work in the fields and in the packing sheds in order to experience for herself what it was like to do the menial labor that many of her friends were doing.

When Dolores was seventeen, her mother took her to Mexico City, a journey which proved to be a turning point in her quest for identity and purpose. She reconnected to her Mexican heritage and gained perspective on the North American culture and the injustices suffered by Latinos in this country. She returned to the United States with a deepened sense of ethnic pride and a strong commitment to working for social justice by helping those less fortunate than herself.[88]

## An activist is born

Shortly after graduating from high school, Dolores married her Irish boyfriend, Ralph Head. Their brief and troubled marriage left Dolores with two children, and as a single parent she enrolled at the College of the Pacific in Stockton to get a teaching degree. She began teaching, but soon quit her job, offering this explanation: "I couldn't stand seeing kids come to class hungry and needing shoes. I thought I could do more by organizing farmworkers than by trying to teach their hungry children."[89] Richard A. García has suggested that Dolores' decision was motivated by her disillusionment with the traditional Hispanic women's organizations that she had joined, the frustrations of being a single parent, and the limited intellectual stimulation provided by her overcrowded classroom.[90] Dolores was looking for something that would satisfy her need to make a difference in her students' lives and would satisfy a deeper

---

88 García, Richard. 64.
89 Schiff 302.
90 García, Richard. 64.

social vocation that was driving her.

In 1955 Dolores was recruited by Fred Ross Sr., the head of the Community Service Organization (CSO) in Stockton, to work on organizing at the grassroots level in order to improve the lives of low-income residents of towns and cities. The CSO helped communities work toward increasing the number of Spanish-speaking police officers, medical personnel, and public servants. They established community centers and lobbied for improvements in services such as sewer systems, garbage collection and electric companies.

While working at CSO, Dolores married Ventura Huerta and had five more children. While struggling to raise her family, she commuted daily to Sacramento to lobby for bills that would improve conditions for poor immigrants and low-income workers. Her negotiating skills became almost legendary, and Dolores "took pride in her successful invasion of the male world of Sacramento politics."[91] In 1961 alone, fifteen bills for which she had lobbied were approved by the California legislature.

Such intense activity took its toll on her marriage, and that year she and Ventura Huerta separated and he initiated a bitter custody battle. While fighting for custody of her children in court and making frequent calls on legislators, Dolores also was trying to support her mother, who was dying of cancer. Meanwhile, at the CSO she had met her professional soul mate, César Chávez, who agreed with her position that the CSO was too focused on urban problems and that they needed to make organizing farmworkers a high priority.[92]

This was a necessary step because of the limited scope of the New Deal legislation enacted in the mid-1930s. Laws such as

91 Rose 102.
92 Schiff 313.

the National Labor Relations Act, the Wagner Act, and the Fair Labor Standards Act protected workers' rights to form unions and negotiate for fair wages and better working conditions, but these laws specifically excluded agricultural laborers. In the 30s and 40s, in the wake of the mechanization of agriculture, many small farms were combined into extensive tracts of land bought by large corporations. Thus, impersonal agribusinesses replaced family-run farms, and the displaced farmworkers could not satisfy the demand for cheap labor. To ease the shortage of workers, the U.S. government set up the Bracero program with cooperation from the Mexican government. Named for the Spanish term for manual laborer, this program lasted from 1942 to 1964 and provided a continuous supply of Mexican laborers willing to accept low wages and miserable working conditions. The protections mandated by law were not enforced, and the braceros often were used to break strikes.[93] For these reasons, Dolores has been a strong critic of the Bracero program and any similar legislation that provides temporary work permits. She would prefer that Mexican workers receive green cards and eventually have the option of applying for citizenship.

When the CSO refused to support the formation of a farmworkers' union in the spring of 1962, César Chávez quit his job and with Dolores' help he took on the daunting task of creating the National Farm Workers Association (NFWA), the precursor to United Farm Workers (UFW). Chávez persuaded her to continue working for the CSO in Stockton until they had recruited more dues-paying members to the NFWA. For several years she maintained a backbreaking schedule, holding down two jobs while being paid for one. Eventually she had to leave the CSO and move to Delano in order to be closer to the central organization. Since she couldn't afford housing of her own, she and six of her children moved into the crowded house that Chávez shared with his wife and their eight

---

93 Ibid. 303-306.

children, and they picked grapes to finance their union activities.

Dolores and César drove to every town and labor camp in the San Joaquin valley, knocking on doors and visiting workers in the fields, trying to persuade them to join the union. They held their first union convention in September of 1962 in an abandoned movie theater in Fresno, and by 1964 they had enrolled 1000 members.[94] They chose as their symbol the Aztec eagle, still visible on some ancient ruins in central Mexico: a black eagle, drawn with right-angled stair-step wings, inside a white circle on a red background. The successful utilization of this symbol parallels the Chicano Movement's adaptation of the name Aztlán (land of the Aztecs) for their figurative, non-geographic homeland, and illustrates the power that such historically significant cultural symbols have to represent hope and solidarity.

One of their first attempts at a strike was with flower workers in 1965, but their efforts were initially unsuccessful because of strike breakers brought in from a town in Mexico. The union offered these undocumented workers full benefits, which were rejected at first, but eventually the organizers persuaded all of the workers to join the union and they managed to negotiate a modest increase in wages.[95] This exemplifies the way the union managed to increase their influence by building alliances rather than excluding people from their organization.

A year later the union gained national attention when they joined with Filipino workers and the Agricultural Workers Organizing Committee (AWOC) for the Delano grape strike. NFWA and AWOC soon merged to form the United Farm Workers Organizing Committee (UFWOC), later shortened to UFW.[96] The grape growers tried to undermine the strikers by hiring thugs to

---

94 May 43-44.
95 Schiff 321-322.
96 May 44.

beat up the picketers, drive them off the road, and spray them with chemicals. They pressured the police to arrest the picketers and to use force in order to control demonstrations. In 1966 Dolores participated in what she called a pilgrimage, a 300-mile march from Delano to Sacramento. By the time most of the marchers had arrived at the state capital, one of the growers had agreed to talk to the union. Dolores negotiated that contract and subsequent agreements with the rest of the growers in 1970, thus becoming the first woman and the first Mexican American to negotiate union contracts with California growers.[97] The 1970 contracts were one result of a very successful national boycott of grapes that Dolores orchestrated. In order to expand the boycott from the state to the national level, she had moved to New York for two years so that she could network with other groups. This move split up her family and created additional stress.

Dolores was juggling multiple roles in the UFW. Besides lobbying and organizing boycotts, she dealt with personnel issues and recruited new members to the union. In 1973 when the UFW contracts with the growers began to expire, the Teamsters began to pressure workers to join their union. Since the Teamsters had influence with the growers, many workers were fired if they didn't sign up with the Teamsters, which caused a drastic reduction in the number of UFW members. The Teamsters and the growers signed "sweetheart contracts" that did not provide protection to the workers. Dolores worked diligently to persuade the laborers to reject the unfavorable contracts and return to the UFW. Eventually she succeeded in winning back all the previous contracts, but their struggle continued and violence against UFW members persisted as well.

Largely due to Dolores' tireless efforts, the Agricultural Labor Relations Act was passed in California in 1975, establishing the collective bargaining rights of farmworkers. Later that year she

97 Schiff 322-329 and Pérez 34.

succeeded in her efforts to ban the *cortito,* a short hoe that forced laborers to work for hours in a bent position, and which had become a symbol of the growers' arrogant and oppressive attitude toward the workers. She also promoted the "Five Cents for Fairness" campaign to disseminate the idea of paying five cents more for a basket of strawberries so that workers could receive better pay and health coverage. Her lobbying led to the first medical and pension plan for the laborers, the first credit union, higher wages, more affordable housing, and safer working conditions. Dolores filed a lawsuit against the use of DDT in the fields and was accused of perjury because of her heartfelt testimony, which was later proven to be all too true. "The pesticide manufacturers push pesticides like they're candy through their marketing... [Many growers] don't know what they're using," she explained, "and they overdose, using more pesticides than they have to."[98] Her struggle to ban DDT and other pesticides has made produce safer for consumers as well as having improved working conditions for laborers.

## Nonviolent tactics meet violent reprisals

Over the years, members of the UFW developed a full range of nonviolent tactics: boycotts, picketing, marches, peaceful demonstrations, and lobbying politicians. Even when Chávez was confronted with violence by his opponents, he steadfastly followed Mahatma Gandhi's philosophy of passive resistance. One of Gandhi's most effective tactics was fasting, and Chávez utilized this tactic to call national attention to his cause. During one of Chávez's most publicized fasts in February of 1968, he ate *nothing* for 25 days, and his weight plunged from 175 to 140 pounds, much to the detriment of his health. Although Gandhi's success with this tactic inspired Chávez, the concept of self-inflicted suffering for a cause is prevalent in Mexican culture, as illustrated by the large

98 "Farm Workers on the Front Lines" 1/2.

number of Mexicans who crawl on their knees for long distances in order to plead for some intervention by the Virgin of Guadalupe, the indigenous representation of the Virgin Mary.

One motivation for the UFW's nonviolent policy was their concern for the safety of picketers and demonstrators, many of whom brought their children with them. Unfortunately, according to Dolores, during the years of protest there were five union members who died from beatings or suspicious accidents. She knew all five victims personally, and she still mourns the loss of these people, whom she calls martyrs to the cause. In 1988, when Dolores was 58 years old, she suffered a brutal assault by a San Francisco policeman during a peaceful demonstration, resulting in four broken ribs and a shattered spleen that had to be removed. Even from her hospital bed she managed to effect change, because after this event the San Francisco Police Department was forced to change its policies regarding crowd control and police discipline.[99]

### Stormy relationships, criticism, and other hardships

Dolores' thirty-year alliance with Chávez provided the UFW with many historic victories, but their professional relationship was often stormy. Chávez usually treated Dolores as an equal, but he actually "fired" her once. She was back on the job the next day as if nothing had happened. They fought about specific strategies for strengthening the UFW and about how the union should participate in politics. Chávez was leery of the political process and uncomfortable speaking with government officials. He did not approve of her lobbying tactics, but he had to concede that they were effective. Chávez was conservative in his attitude toward family life, and he criticized Dolores' unconventional lifestyle, particularly her two divorces and her nontraditional attitude toward

---

99 DHF website.

parenting. Chávez was not pleased when Dolores began seeing his brother Richard, and he was irritated even more when she began "cohabiting" with him. Dolores had four more children while living with Richard Chávez, and the couple eventually married. Dolores' third marriage has proven to be more stable and supportive than her first two, but even Richard has had problems with her activism. Dolores has been criticized by her partners, her father and brother, and by other traditional members of society. Moreover, she has had the additional burden of having to deal with her own feelings of guilt and maternal desire to be with her children.

Dolores was pregnant and/or caring for young ones for more than three decades, since there are 26 years between the oldest and youngest of her eleven children. She usually had to depend on family and union members to care for some of her offspring, while she brought others along on her trips. She received irregular support from her husbands and a subsistence-level stipend from the union, so she frequently had to accept temporary translation jobs, substitute teaching, and even brief stints working in the fields in order to make ends meet. She had offers of more lucrative full-time positions, but she chose to live in poverty so that she could devote her time to the union and relate more effectively to the farmworkers' condition. The union's financial situation was so dire that she sometimes lacked the essential tools for effective organizing: reliable transportation and means of communication. She once complained to Chávez that she had "no car, no typewriter, no phone."[100]

Besides having to deal with family obligations and poverty, Dolores had to contend with the downdraft of *machismo*, a belief held by some traditional Mexicans that women should be subservient to men. Sometimes male farmworkers refused to meet with a female organizer or they would walk out of meetings when she tried to speak. Early on, Dolores resorted to utilizing her 100 Rose 100.

second husband (Ventura Huerta) and her brother as fronts for her organizing activities. As she gained confidence, Dolores tried to educate the men about the advances being made by women, and she even started making checkmarks on a ledger every time one of them made a sexist statement in a meeting. As proof that she was making headway, one of Chávez's security guards once told her, "Dolores, when you walk in the room, the whole climate changes."[101]

### Dolores as a feminist

Dolores' mother inspired her with her independent thinking, entrepreneurial spirit, and compassion for others. Alicia Chávez set an egalitarian tone in her household, demanding the same help with chores from both sons and daughters. According to Richard A. García, there was "no sexual discrimination in her home and consequently no sense of inferiority, no encouragement to accept a secondary role in her life and later in her work with the union... no contradictory masculine/feminine messages from her mother."[102] Such equality in her upbringing probably contributed to Dolores' disregard for the need to establish a feminine mystique. Her simple clothes and straightforward manner convey a message of self-confidence and unadorned womanly strength.

Dolores initially considered the women's liberation movement of the 1960s to be a white middle-class organization, as did many low-income women and women of color. White middle-class women were perceived as being focused on their right to go back to school or enter the workforce, whereas poor women could not afford college and always had held jobs to help support their families. However, some feminists were sensitive to these issues, and when Dolores was in New York organizing the grape

101 Schiff 335.
102 García, Richard. 60-61.

boycott, she received support from some prominent feminists, including Gloria Steinem. Dolores realized that there was an important connection between the exploitation of farmworkers and of women in general, and that feminists could be valuable allies. When she returned to California, she consciously began to challenge gender discrimination within the UFW. She became a founding member of the Feminist Majority Foundation, an early participant in the National Organization of Women, and an organizer of the Coalition for Labor Union Women. She has given rousing speeches at many feminist demonstrations and marches, such as the March for Women's Lives in 2004. For two years she traveled around the United States promoting the Feminization of Power campaign in order to encourage Latinas to seek political office, and the result was a substantial increase in the number of female candidates who won election at the local, state and federal levels.[103]

In her speeches and interviews, Dolores often repeats her opinion that women should make their own decisions, take credit for the important work they do, and believe in themselves. Women should follow their dreams, according to her, and not let anyone stand in the way. "Everybody has a gift," she has said, "and we've got to figure out what that gift is and the things that they really like to do are the things they need to pursue."[104]

## The Dolores Huerta Foundation and the Weaving Movements campaign

After years of backbreaking work in the fields, extreme fasts that taxed his health, and steadfast devotion to nonviolence while

103 DHF website and Schiff 334-335.
104 Drake 3/3.

facing brutal repression, César Chávez died of a heart attack at the age of 66. At Chávez's funeral in 1993, Dolores and other union leaders took a vow to continue the struggle. Dolores has been true to her word, although she did not take his place as president of the UFW; she chose to endorse Arturo Rodríguez instead, and to broaden the spectrum of her own activities. In 2003 she resigned from the UFW, but she still identifies herself as the Co-founder, Secretary Treasurer, and First Vice President Emeritus of the UFW.

Unfortunately, Dolores took a forced hiatus from her work in the year 2000, when she was hospitalized for months with a brain aneurysm and doctors feared that she would not survive. Her slow and painful recovery process included having to re-learn how to walk, talk, and even eat. And yet, in a remarkable demonstration of her fighting spirit, in 2001 she led UFW members on a 165-mile, 11-day march from Bakersfield to Sacramento. The union was trying to pressure Governor Gray Davis to sign a bill requiring growers to agree to arbitration if negotiations with farmworkers broke down. The governor eventually signed the bill in September of 2002.[105]

That same year Dolores received the Puffin/Nation prize for Creative Citizenship, and she used the $100,000 award to establish the Dolores Huerta Foundation (DHF). Dolores continues to serve as president of her foundation on a volunteer basis, and her youngest daughter, Camila Chávez, is the Executive Director.[106] Their mission is "to create a network of organized communities pursuing social justice through systemic and structural transformation." They are focusing on four priority areas: 1) health and environment, 2) education, 3) youth development, and 4) economic development.

---

105 Schiff 338-339.

106 Unless otherwise noted, all quotes and information on the DHF comes from the DHF website. There are multiple links on the site, so I was not able to print out a document with meaningful page numbers.

Dolores and her staff travel around the country giving workshops on grassroots organization, leadership development, and policy advocacy. She frequently speaks to student groups and civic organizations, advocating for the rights of workers, immigrants, women, children, and the LGBT[107] community. In 2009, Dolores delivered the plenary keynote speech at the 21st National Conference on LGBT Equality: Creating Change, which was organized by the National Gay and Lesbian Task Force. Besides mentioning her own connections to the LGBT community, she emphasized the need to educate ourselves about each other's movements and to be informed about the issues that affect us all.

A year later, as part of her ongoing effort to build alliances with organizations that are promoting social justice, Dolores celebrated her 80th birthday by launching the "Weaving Movements" campaign at a fundraising concert for the DHF. This campaign calls on progressive leaders and human rights activists around the nation to coordinate their activities and rally around a common goal. "I think the Weaving Movements campaign has been successful," Dolores told me. "We have a lot more people working together. For instance, the Latinos working for the DREAM Act[108] worked very closely with the LGBT community, and we have labor unions now that are working with other groups."[109] The DHF will continue for as long as there are people willing to get involved. "The kind of work that we do is very difficult," Dolores told me. "The organizing takes a lot of patience and it's very time-consuming, so hopefully

107 Lesbian, Gay, Bisexual, and Transgender. Currently it is more prevalent to add Q, for Queer, but since Dolores says LGBT, that is what I have used here.
108 DREAM Act: the Development, Relief, and Education for Alien Minors Act, which puts a hold on deportations of undocumented students.
109 García, Kay. "Interview with Dolores Huerta."

we'll inspire enough people who will want to continue it for a long time."[110]

On the local level, the DHF encourages communities in California to form neighborhood organizations called *Vecinos Unidos* (United Neighbors) in order to foster change in their area. Members are taught how to use nonviolent tactics and elicit the cooperation of public officials in order to influence local, state and national issues and work toward a more egalitarian society. The various neighborhood groups coalesce to form a social justice network that develops "indigenous leadership." According to their website, "The Vecinos Unidos model proves that the working poor and immigrants have the potential leadership to resolve issues.... By working together, they take collective responsibility for their lives and their communities."

Recently The Hermes Music Foundation collaborated with DHF to produce a CD, *"Claro que se puede"* (Of course we can) as a fundraiser for Dolores' organization. With help from performing artists Carlos Santana, Willie Nelson, Los Lonely Boys, and several others, Dolores is using music to disseminate her ideas. Some of the songs on the disc are reminiscent of the protest songs of Bob Dylan, Pete Seeger, and John Lennon.

### Dolores' legacy

Dolores continues to be a strong role model for Latinas, many of whom have been inspired by her leadership and her courageous activism. Seeing a woman stand up for herself and for others meant a lot to Lupe Ortiz, a union member who commented, "We could see she was always out in front, and she would talk back. She wasn't scared of anything."[111] Besides helping to pass legislation to

110 Ibid.
111 Quoted in Pérez 7-8.

protect agricultural workers' rights, Dolores managed to include many daily necessities in the contracts she negotiated with growers, such as toilets in the fields, along with soap, water and paper towels; cold drinking water with individual paper cups; rest periods; and paid holidays. These essentials that most people take for granted made working conditions more bearable and forced the growers to treat the laborers as people, rather than beasts of burden. In addition, Dolores worked with César Chávez to create a service center to coordinate the building of low-income housing throughout the country, and to establish Radio Campesina, a radio network that broadcasts to farmworkers in California, Washington and Arizona.[112]

One of her most significant achievements was effecting a change in the national attitude toward farmworkers. She always promotes respect for people who work in the fields or at other menial tasks. In 2003 when she spoke to the students in one of the elementary schools named after her, she told the children, many of whom came from farmworker families, "Your parents and grandparents do the most sacred work in the world. They feed everybody."[113]

Another accomplishment that gives her pride is Dolores' ability to help progressive candidates get elected. Asked why she doesn't run for office herself, she replied, "As an organizer I believe I can do a lot more by getting other people to run and by supporting good candidates."[114] She helped Robert F. Kennedy win the 1968 Democratic Presidential Primary in California, and he recognized her contribution to his campaign just minutes before he was shot. In 1992, her work with the Feminization of Power campaign contributed to the election of the largest number of female legislators in the history of California, including the largest number

112 Aledo 1/6.
113 Quoted in Schiff 340.
114 Quoted in Aledo 4/6.

of Latina and African American candidates. Dolores has worked to elect President Bill Clinton, Senator Hillary Clinton, Congressman Ron Dellums, Governor Jerry Brown, and Congresswoman Hilda Solis, among others.[115]

For his first presidential campaign, Barack Obama borrowed the slogan she created, *"Sí, se puede,"* and used its English rendition "Yes, we can" to help inspire his followers. During the ceremony when he placed the Medal of Freedom around her neck, the President remarked, "Dolores was very gracious when I told her I had stolen her slogan…. Knowing her, I'm pleased that she let me off easy – because Dolores does not play."[116]

Even though many people are still unaware of Dolores' important contributions to society, she is becoming more recognized for her achievements. According to Karenna Gore Schiff, "she was recently surprised to see her own face on T-shirts commemorating La Causa, right alongside César's. 'It's because of the Latinas,' she told me. 'They want to see a woman's face.'"[117] Moreover, Dolores has been awarded honorary doctorates by universities across the nation, and given prestigious appointments by the California university system. She has held positions as a University of California Regent and as a University of Southern California instructor in charge of lecturing on community organizing.[118]

When asked what legacy she hopes to leave, Dolores responded, "I think my greatest life achievements are my children because they are so great…. They have been able to raise themselves and do great things."[119] Her children's professions are attorney, paralegal,

---

115 DHF website.
116 "Remarks by the President at Presidential Medal of Freedom Ceremony"
117 Schiff 340.
118 Aledo 1/6.
119 Ibid. 5/6.

medical doctor, performing artist, therapist, chef, filmmaker, nurse, teacher, and two administrators.[120] Later, in reference to her organizing activities, she mentioned how rewarding it was for her to see all the progress that has been made and to see that somebody's life was saved because he was able to get an operation. That helps her realize how important her work is. [121]

There are still enormous challenges facing women and immigrants in the United States. While rejoicing in the advances made by women in graduate school and some professions, Dolores points out that women still lag behind in the corporate world. She also is concerned that the war on terror has created a lack of funding for education, health care and infrastructure that disproportionately affects Latino children. Furthermore, she is concerned that the specter of terrorism has been used to disguise attacks on immigrants. Specifically, she has criticized the "wall being built along the Mexican border, even though we've never had any terrorists come in through the Mexican border."[122]

### Lessons to share: an education of the heart

"One thing I've learned," Dolores has said, "is that having tremendous fears and anxieties is normal…. By doing whatever causes your anxiety, you overcome the fear, and strengthen your emotional, spiritual, activist muscles."[123] According to Dolores, in order to be successful as an activist, one must: establish a strong sense of identity, develop a sense of pride, always maintain the value of service to others, and remain self-reflective and true to oneself.[124] Moreover, she asserts, you have to remember that the

120 Schiff 340.
121 Aledo 5/6.
122 Ibid. 2/6.
123 Quoted in Chávez 240.
124 These recommendations, which have been summarized and

74

power is in your person. It's inside you, and together with other people, you can make a difference. "But ...nobody is going to do it for you," she insists, "If you don't get out there and try to solve your own problems, it's never going to change."[125]

Dolores' other recommendations for aspiring activists include:

1)   Find politicians who will fight for your cause, and make it easy for them to help you (by arranging boycotts, marches, and peaceful demonstrations).

2)   Keep your message simple ("Don't buy grapes," as opposed to a long list of growers to boycott.)

3)   Teach people how to further their own causes, and allow them to bring the issues to the negotiating table themselves.

4)   Lobby extensively at the grassroots level because politicians will pay attention to their constituents.

5)   Look for opportunities. If a law passes that doesn't apply, lobby for the passage of a bill that does apply.[126]

Besides these recommendations, there are other things that can be learned by simply watching Dolores in action. She leads by example, convinces through persuasion, and has not been afraid to put herself in confrontational and even dangerous situations. She has widened the spectrum of her activities in order to champion all marginalized and oppressed people in this country, and her all-inclusive attitude has won her numerous allies and increased the momentum of her organization.

One of Dolores' causes is the reform of our public school system.

---

paraphrased here, are included in the article by Richard García, on page 66.
125 Suarez 4/4.
126 Condensed and adapted from Aledo 2/6 – 5/6.

"Education is the soul of the nation," according to Dolores. "We must have an education of the heart, so after graduation, students come back and give back to the community."[127] Dolores is concerned about the lack of information about Latinos in the curriculum, which gives Latino children the impression that they are not part of society. She stresses the need for teachers to be informed about the contributions made by Latinos, and for students to be taught in both English and Spanish. Dolores criticizes what she calls our "elimination society," in which low-income students who can't compete are filtered out of our schools and then channeled toward prison instead of toward college.[128] In order for things to change, Dolores emphasizes the need for collective action:

> We have to get together and fight to improve our educational system. Our children are being denied the quality education that they need because of the No Child Left Behind[129] program and the elimination of bilingual education. Latinos and African-Americans have the highest suspension rates and the highest expulsion rates. And it's almost a crime to tell them to go to college when the fees are so high and there's no money for them to go.[130]

Dolores believes that having positive role models can make a difference in the lives of young Latinos. "We have so many Latinos in the U.S. now, and our numbers are growing, and yet there's so much negativity about our community because of immigration issues and other problems. So I think it's important for young

---

127 "Dolores Huerta Speaks at UCLA Graduation."
128 "Dolores Huerta on Education."
129 No Child Left Behind is a federal law enacted in 2001 that requires states to develop assessments in basic skills and give these assessments to all students at select grade levels in order to receive federal school funding.
130 García, Kay. "Interview with Dolores Huerta."

Latinos to have some good role models."[131]

## Dolores as a leader: transforming herself and her campaigns

Dolores has overcome adversity, contributed to positive change, set precedents, served as a role model, and maintained her connection to the Latino community. Not only has she done these things, but she has continued to do them for almost sixty years. In 2011, at the age of 81, Dolores marched on a picket line for two hours in support of the Hilton Long Beach Hotel workers who were fired for being whistle-blowers. On May Day of 2012 she spoke at a rally for Waste and Recycle Workers, and as of 2013 she was still accepting speaking engagements across the country.

When asked in 2013 what keeps her going, Dolores replied, "Well, there's a lot of work to be done, and it's not going to get done unless we get out there and do it."[132] Regarding her plans for the future, Dolores has a simple blueprint: "Just to keep on working."[133]

The criticism leveled at Dolores for not being a traditional mother may concern some people. However, it can be beneficial to be introduced to social activism at a young age, and all of Dolores' children have affirmed their mother's choices by participating in her organizations in various ways, some quite extensively. Regardless of one's opinion of nontraditional parenting, the fact is that Dolores is a human being, complete with flaws, and yet she has managed to improve the lives of countless numbers of people. Thus, she is a good example of the concept that ordinary people can do extraordinary things if they make a firm commitment to a cause.

---

131 Ibid.
132 Ibid.
133 Ibid.

Part of Dolores' legacy is the convincing way in which she demonstrated that one woman's activism could have a profound effect on a sociopolitical movement, and the same kind of involvement could provide a path to self-determination. In addition, she has illustrated clearly that the sexist marginalization of women is an impediment to the advancement of society and, most ironically, to progressive causes. While negotiating contracts, Dolores had to deal with the owners of huge tracts of land, who were reminiscent of Mexican *"hacendados"* (owners of large estates) in their arrogant attitude toward workers and women. Even within her own union, Dolores had to contend with the undermining force of *machismo,* as well as the lack of daycare and other support systems that make professional activity feasible for modern women.

Dolores has engaged in a continuous transformation of herself and her organizations, responding to the changing realities of each constituency she represents and thus revitalizing her campaigns as well as the national dialogue. Therefore, her complex identity cannot be revealed by a simple list of what could appear to be contradictory adjectives --unassuming/self-confident, sensitive/passionate, flexible/tough-minded, intuitive/intelligent, Mexican/American, feminine/masculine-- all of which apply to her. Rather, her individuality lies in the ways in which she has combined these qualities within herself, calling upon them at differing times and utilizing each one in a constantly evolving way. Nonetheless, her rallying cry "Sí se puede" allows us to appreciate what is at the unchanging core of her being, and besides helping to define her spirit, this slogan will serve as inspiration for future generations.

§ § §

# Bibliography

## Books and Book Chapters

Chávez, Alicia. "Dolores Huerta and The United Farm Workers." *Latina Legacies: Identity, Biography, and Community*. Eds. Vicki L. Ruiz and Virginia Sanchez Korral. Oxford University Press, 2005, 240-254.

Pérez, Frank. *Contemporary Hispanic Americans: Dolores Huerta*. Austin, Texas: Raintree Steck-Vaughn Publishers, 1996.

Rose, Margaret. "César Chávez and Dolores Huerta: Partners in 'La Causa'." *César Chávez: A Brief Biography with Documents*. Ed. Richard W. Etulain.New York: PALGRAVE, 2002, 95-107.

Schiff, Karenna Gore. "Dolores Huerta." *Lighting the Way: Nine Women Who Changed Modern America*. New York: Miramax Books, 2005.

## Articles, Interviews, and Web Pages (web pages accessed Jan-Feb 2013)

Aledo, Milagros and Maria C. Alvarado. "Dolores Huerta at Seventy-Five: Still Empowering Communities." *Harvard Journal of Hispanic Policy*. Volume 18, 2005-2006.

Alvarado, Victoria G. "Dolores Huerta." *Mujeres de Conciencia/ Women of Conscience*. Mountain View, CA: Floricanto Press, 2007.

"Biografía de Dolores Huerta." UFW website. http://www.ufw.org.

Dolores Huerta Foundation website. http://www.doloreshuerta. org.

"Dolores Huerta on Education." http://www.youtube.com.

"Dolores Huerta Speaks at UCLA Graduation."16 Jun 2009. http://www.youtube.com.

Drake, Susan Samuels. "Dolores Huerta: A Role Model for Any Age." http://www.seniorwomen.com.

"Farm Workers on the Front Lines: An Interview with Dolores Huerta." 31 Mar 1997. CorpWatch website. http://www.corpwatch. org.

García, Kay S. "Interview with Dolores Huerta." Recorded 30 Jul 2013. Unpublished.

Garcia, Richard A. "Dolores Huerta: Woman, Organizer, and Symbol." *California History*. Vol. 72, No. 1, Spring 1993, 56-71.

Gehrke, Joel. "Obama took 'Yes, we can' from Dolores Huerta." The Washington Examiner. 29 May 2012. http://washingtonexaminer.com.

Mexican Embassy website. http://embamex.sre.gob.mx/canada.

Oliva, Flor de María. "La Causa de Dolores Huerta." *Santa Fe New Mexican*, New Mexico, 3 Mar 2003, C-1.

"Remarks by the President at Presidential Medal of Freedom Ceremony." http://www.whitehouse.gov.

Suarez, Ray. "Dolores Huerta Calls Herself 'a Born-Again Feminist'." PBS Interview with Ray Suarez. 30 May 2012. http://video.pbs.org.

# Jorge Ramos

25th Anniversary photos as Univisión anchor
Below: On set with co-anchor María Elena Salinas

Making a point during a
heated discussion

Questioning President about
immigration reform

## Chapter Three

## Jorge Ramos: News Anchor and Advocate

"I remember my first afternoon in this country perfectly. My plane landed in Los Angeles. I was almost broke, but as I walked out of the airport carrying all of my belongings, I felt free. And I smiled. Thirty years later, all that is left to say is: Thank you, thank you, thank you."

--Jorge Ramos

In January of 1983, a skinny, scared Mexican arrived alone in Los Angeles with just a suitcase and his guitar. Twenty-six years later, that same slender Mexican –no longer scared, but somewhat embarrassed and humbled by the attention—was inducted into the Broadcasting and Cable Hall of Fame. For those of you who do not watch news in Spanish, Jorge Ramos often has been identified as the Latino Walter Cronkite, but millions of viewers who watch the Spanish-language channel *Univisión* might understand the comparison better if Mr. Cronkite were identified as the Anglo Jorge Ramos.

Since 1986, Jorge[134] and his co-anchor María Elena Salinas have

134 I ask for Jorge's and the reader's understanding in regard to the

82

been reporting the news every evening on *Noticiero Univisión* (Newscast of *Univisión*). Their program, which is broadcast to affiliates throughout the United States and in 13 Latin American countries, has attracted an ever-increasing audience of over two million people.[135] He is considered to be a representative of Latino perspectives as well as an ardent advocate of immigration reform and other causes. He has contributed substantial amounts of his own money to scholarships for immigrants, and he publicly urges others to make donations.

Besides interviewing dozens of world leaders for his programs and moderating presidential debates, Jorge has borne witness to many of the world's most significant events. He was present for the tearing down of the Berlin Wall, and while doing his report he grabbed a hammer and chisel in order to chip away at the cement himself. He was almost killed on three occasions: once by an erupting volcano, and twice by aircraft malfunctions that prompted emergency landings. He was on site soon after an earthquake struck Mexico City, where he reported on the government's lack of preparation and its failure to enforce building standards. He has traveled to cover five wars, countless floods and hurricanes, and the aftermath of the tragic events of 9/11.

Jorge has been interviewed on all of the major English-language broadcasting networks and, as a sure sign of his success, he was impersonated on Comedy Central's *The Colbert Report* in August of 2008. Stephen Colbert's Hispanic persona, Esteban Colberto, greeted his guest as the anchor of the extremely popular *Noticiero Univisión*, roughly translated by Colberto as "Let's Invade America."

---

use of Jorge's first name in this chapter. I have chosen to use his first name because I am writing about his personal story as well as his career, and I wish to help the reader identify with him.
135 Martínez 1/7. Numbers after articles found online indicate the page number on the print-out/total number of pages, as a general indication of where to find the information in the article.

Jorge should be commended, according to his host, for "his gravitas, his balls, and his power over *las chicas*."[136]

In 2012, Jorge appeared in person on *The Colbert Report*, and the host made the mistake of insisting that undocumented immigrants are criminals. Ignoring Colbert's mischievous smile, Jorge vehemently defended immigrants without papers, citing their contributions to society and contrasting them with truly-criminal war profiteers. "I don't have a comeback for that," conceded Colbert, "so we'll probably have to edit it out of the interview."[137] After that, Jorge smiled and switched to a lighter vein for the rest of the interview.

In addition to reporting the news, Jorge hosts a Sunday morning political talk show called *Al Punto* (To the Point), during which he analyzes the week's top stories and interviews important newsmakers, catching the attention of almost a million weekend viewers. He interviewed Sonia Sotomayor at her workplace in January of 2013. Although he did not manage to get her to express her views on gun control or any other issue before the Supreme Court, he did get her to dance with him, which was probably the first time anyone danced salsa in the Supreme Court Building.

In a dramatic change to personal and network policy, Jorge agreed in 2013 to a joint venture with ABC News: the creation of a new network called *Fusion* to provide Latinos with culturally relevant news and information in English. According to *The Washington Post*, "Ramos calls *Fusion* 'an experiment' - but if it is successful, it could become an economic, cultural and political force."[138] Besides being an acknowledgement that a growing number of Latinos are more proficient in English than in Spanish, this new network is an example of a dynamic tendency toward

---

136 Ibid. 5/7.
137 "The Colbert Report."
138 Roig-Franzia and Wallsten 1/6.

cultural hybridization, as opposed to the more static polarization of Spanish-only versus English-only. Moreover, *Fusion* gives Jorge a chance to serve as a cultural ambassador, sharing Latino perspectives and insights with people of all backgrounds.

A brief sampling of all the awards and recognitions bestowed upon Jorge includes: nine Emmy Awards for excellence in journalism, culminating in the Lifetime Achievement Award given to him and his co-anchor in 2012; the John F. Hogan Distinguished Service Award from the Radio and Television Digital News Association, also in 2012; and, in recognition of his efforts to help young people overcome prejudice and discrimination, he was given the 2002 Ron Brown Award by the National Child Labor Committee.

To his loyal viewers, Jorge is like family, appearing in their living rooms every weeknight for the last couple of decades. Although he sometimes is treated like a star, he doesn't act like one, and many Latinos feel that he is just like them, trying to get ahead through hard work and perseverance. He's simply a "down-to-earth dude," as a bookstore owner called him, after a book signing at which he sold 1,300 of Jorge's books.[139] Jorge has a slim 5'7" frame, silver hair, olive skin, and blue-green eyes that occasionally sparkle with amusement but most often are fixed on the camera with intense seriousness. He looks a lot like Anderson Cooper, and at a recent photo op of the two of them together, photographers joked about not knowing which one was Jorge. He hates to be told that he doesn't look Latino, because his Mexican identity is very important to him, but he accepted the photographers' jokes with a self-deprecating laugh and a shrug of his shoulders.

Besides anchoring for *Univisión*, Jorge has written eleven books, some of which have become bestsellers; he writes a weekly column that is distributed by the New York Times to more than forty newspapers in the United States and Latin America, and he

---

139 "The Anchor" 1/3.

provides daily commentary for the *Radio Univisión* network. His long hours and frequent travels have taken a toll on his personal relationships, particularly in regard to the women in his life. The tabloid press has made an effort to portray him as a ladies' man, but he rejects that image and has blamed his two divorces on the demands of his profession and the careers of his wives. In a recent book, however, he takes responsibility for having caused his divorces. Nonetheless, he is a dedicated father who has made a concerted effort to spend time with his two children, Paola and Nicolás, whom he mentions frequently in his books, in interviews, and when he is accepting awards. He calls himself the "family driver," since he chauffeurs his children around to water polo and other activities. He manages to play soccer every Saturday, he never wears jewelry or a watch, and whenever possible, he avoids wearing a tie.

His nose has been broken three times —during birth by forceps, during a soccer match, and during a basketball game— and the surgical repairs have left him unable to smell all but the strongest of odors, and able to taste only the spiciest of foods. Usually, when one or more senses are lacking, the other senses intensify. In compensation for his lack of taste and smell, I would say he has developed a remarkable sense of adventure, an acute sense of sociopolitical responsibility, and a disarming sense of humor. This latter sense was put to an extreme test when he was asked by Jaime Bayly in a televised interview if he, like Bayly, had become impotent after the birth of his two children. Jorge replied that he would provide the interviewer with a moment of awkward silence —a tactic they had joked about earlier— so his host would know that he was wrong about that.[140]

Jorge is considered a new breed of journalist in that he combines reporting the news with advocating for causes. He does not favor a particular candidate or political party, but he expresses his opinion

140 "Jaime Bayly entrevista a Jorge Ramos."

about issues that are important to him and to his Latino viewers, particularly immigration reform in the United States and the need for stronger and more authentic democracies in Latin America. He has given significant support to the anti-war movement, women's rights, gay rights, prevention of AIDS, and protection of victims of abuse by religious figures. He became a U.S. citizen in time to vote in the historic 2008 election, but as a matter of journalistic principal, he refuses to reveal for which candidates he voted. However, as a dual citizen he continues to vote in Mexico as well, and he has been an outspoken critic of electoral fraud in that country.

### Early years: String Bean, classical guitar, pre-Olympics

Jorge often signs his articles Jorge Ramos Avalos, following the Spanish tradition of using both the paternal and maternal last names. He was born on March 16, 1958, in a suburb of Mexico City.[141] For many years, his family fit the traditional Mexican paradigm, with a father who worked as an architect, a mother who worked at home, four sons, and a daughter. Jorge was named after his father and, as the oldest child, he usually initiated the games and fights with his siblings. Although his father has passed away, Jorge maintains close contact with the rest of his family to this day, but he still believes that they never understood why he left Mexico. He identifies the house they shared as the only place he ever felt at home, and he still remembers the address and phone number, despite his family having changed residences long ago.

His relatives called him *Ejote Verde* (String Bean) because he was skinny, asthmatic, and had a green tint to his skin. Jorge identifies one of his childhood heroes as his maternal grandfather

141 Unless otherwise noted, biographical information in this chapter comes from Jorge Ramos' website, or from his autobiography, *No Borders*. Only direct quotes from these sources will be noted hereafter.

Miguel, whom he describes as a marvelous storyteller who taught him about World War II and the Mexican revolution of 1910. At times when his father didn't have steady work, Jorge would sell nuts from his grandfather's ranch, going door to door in his neighborhood and confronting people on the street. This experience, albeit somewhat embarrassing, helped him develop the ability to approach strangers and ask questions, a skill that would prove very useful when he became a journalist.

As a child, Jorge had two brushes with death. The first time was at a movie theater, when he got a lemon candy caught in his throat and his father had to dangle him by his feet to shake the candy loose. A few years later, he almost drowned off the shore of Acapulco when a strong riptide pulled him out to sea. When he finally made it back to the beach, he was shocked that nobody had noticed his struggle against the tide.

A more prolonged struggle that went unnoticed was at a private Catholic school that Jorge attended, where from kindergarten to his penultimate year of school he was subjected to prejudice and physical beatings by the Benedictine priests who ran the school. He protested so much that he finally was allowed to transfer for his last year of high school. As a result of this mistreatment, he rebelled against Catholicism and all authority figures, including his teachers, parents, and police, and began to identify himself as an existentialist. He felt that he was the only person responsible for his life, as though he had been thrown out into the world with the freedom to do whatever he felt like doing. His search for answers to the existential questions led him to two verbs: to be and to love, which he explains as acting with authenticity (being honest) and trying to love those around him.

In spite of his slight stature, Jorge became an avid athlete, and was allowed to train with the Mexican pre-Olympic track team. He started out as a high jumper, but his height put him at a disadvantage in that event, so he switched to the 400-meter hurdles, and had some success in several national championships. Unfortunately, during treatment of a minor injury he discovered that he had a lumbar vertebra that was not completely closed, which meant that it was too risky for him to continue to train. He had to abandon the Olympic dreams he had harbored since the age of 10. When he told his mother, he cried like never before and, as he put it, something inside him broke. Nevertheless, he still runs to relieve stress, and he recognizes that his athletic competitions helped him learn to control his nerves in front of an audience. Another ambition, to become a professional musician, led to his playing classical guitar for a few audiences, but when he realized that he couldn't express himself completely with music he turned to writing instead.

At the Universidad Iberoamericana in Mexico City, Jorge chose to study Communications, a direct rebellion against his father's desire that he study something "more practical." His mother, Lourdes Avalos, whom he described as having the characteristics of a "silent heroine," pushed him to find meaning in his life beyond the conventional expectations of a typical middle-class family. Lourdes had first rebelled against her controlling husband by refusing to follow his detailed instructions about how to prepare a cup of hot chocolate for him. Later, this rebellion escalated when she began to take university classes along with her children, taking pleasure in encountering them in the hallways of the academic buildings, and engaging in discussions with them about the ideas of Freud, Marx, Nietzche, and other intellectuals.

Jorge credits another two women for inspiring him to pursue his specific profession: the Mexican writer Elena Poniatowska, for her strength, honesty and sensitivity; and the Italian journalist Oriana Fallaci, for her aggressive style of interviewing powerful people.[142]

142 See Poniatowska's *Massacre in Mexico*, and Fallaci's *Interview with History*. Elena Poniatowska's work is discussed in Chapter Six

Later, when he was completing his degree, Jorge recognized the inequalities of Mexican society and the subordinate role of women within his profession. He decided to write his thesis for graduation on "The Woman as Communicator in Commercial Advertising on Mexican Television," in which he utilized concepts presented in Simone de Beauvoir's influential book *The Second Sex.* According to Jorge, he became a fervent advocate of feminism due to a profoundly egalitarian, eight-year relationship that he had with his first girlfriend, named Kuas.

While studying at the university, he no longer received the scholarships that had helped pay for his pre-secondary education, so he was obliged to find work at a travel agency, where he soon acquired a strong desire to travel around the world. Because of this job, his classes, and the long commute by bus and metro across the sprawling city, his days began at 5:00 a.m. and he returned home, dog-tired, around 8:00 p.m. He caught a break when he was offered the opportunity to audition for XEW, an important radio station, where he started working as a research assistant but was soon given the opportunity to report news and conduct interviews on the air. Meanwhile, he was trying to learn about televised reporting, but an earthquake in 1979 had destroyed all the university buildings. His television professor had to hold class in a hastily constructed shelter, where he drew a diagram of a television studio on a piece of cardboard. That was the extent of his television training at the Iberoamericana.

Jorge was able to take advantage of an extraordinary opportunity to try his hand at international reporting in 1981, when President Reagan suffered an attempt on his life. When news of the shooting arrived at XEW, Jorge was the only reporter there who could speak English and also had a passport ready to go. When he arrived at Washington, he had no idea how to gain

---

of this book (i.e. *Latino and Latina Leaders of the 21st Century.*)

entrance to press conferences or to arrange for interviews; he even resorted to taping interviews from his hotel TV set. Eventually he made a breakthrough by following the right nurse around the hospital where Reagan was being treated. She gave him valuable information and saved him from certain failure as a correspondent. Referring to this incident, Jorge writes, "I don't believe in destiny, nor do I believe in luck. I believe in being prepared to take advantage of opportunities that present themselves. I also believe that there is almost never a second chance."[143]

Shortly after this success, Jorge went to work as an investigator for the Televisa news program *60 Minutos* (sixty minutes), which had a reputation for tabloid journalism, but at least it gave him an entrance to television. During an assignment to investigate the eruption of the Chichonal volcano in Chiapas, he and the TV crew barely escaped with their lives after coming as close as they could to the volcano, whose powerful gasses caused an explosion that blew up the exact spot where they had been stuck with their car moments earlier.

The story that really changed his life, however, was his report on the Mexican psyche, in which he critiqued the authoritarian system of the Mexican government. The official party (*Partido Revolucionario Institucional*, or the Institutional Revolutionary Party), known as PRI, had a stranglehold on all mass media, and defying the party was known to end not only careers but also lives. His report was edited beyond recognition in order to present a rosy picture of the status quo, so he quit his job and soon thereafter began preparations for his journey to the United States.

---

143 *No Borders* 54.

## An immigrant in L.A.: from waiting on tables to reporting on local television

For some years, Jorge had been struggling against the oppressive social conventions and institutions in his country, rebelling against all the rules and expectations of his family, the government and the Catholic Church. "The Mexico that I was living in was suffocating me and becoming a dead-end road," he wrote. "I needed air, new ideas, a reason for being, and I was not finding that in Mexico." [144] The decision to leave his family, his long-time sweetheart, his friends and his community was not an easy one, but he was not willing to wait forever for freedom of expression and other civil liberties to be initiated in Mexico when there was a country just north of the border where such freedoms were already established.

In order to enter the United States legally, he applied for a student visa and enrolled in a broadcast journalism program at UCLA. He sold his old VW, packed a suitcase and his guitar and, at the age of 24, flew to L.A. by himself on January 2, 1983. He found a cheap room to rent, which he shared with a series of roommates, and for months he ate rice and noodles that he cooked in a closet. He worked as a waiter at *Chez Louise*, and then at a money-changing and wiring business, where he learned that every year Mexicans send as much as eight billion dollars to their families back home. The office where he worked was in an old theater, so he was able to increase his calories by munching on popcorn and candy. Jorge has written about the extreme loneliness that he felt during this period of his life. His girlfriend Kuas came to visit him twice, but their long-distance relationship failed, partly because of Jorge's reluctance to start a family at a time when he was struggling to jump-start his career.

---

144 Ibid. 45.

When he tried to get work in television, he was told that his accent was so strong that viewers wouldn't be able to understand him, and that he should forget about Spanish-language television because Hispanics were going to assimilate and watch the news in English.[145] His luck changed when Pete Moraga offered him a job as a reporter for KMEX, Channel 34 in Los Angeles, just as he was finishing his program at UCLA. When an earthquake struck Mexico City in 1985, once again he was the only available reporter with a passport ready to go, so he was sent there to cover the disaster. The destruction and countless deaths were overwhelming, but the worst blow was that his inseparable friend and co-worker, Félix, had been crushed in the ruins of the Televisa building where Jorge had worked before emigrating. Jorge surely would have died at his friend's side if he had not left Mexico.

## The move to Miami: a warrior comes out

Denying himself time to grieve, Jorge returned to work and threw himself into investigating and reporting any story that came his way. Within a year of being hired at KMEX he was offered a job hosting their morning news show along with Felipe "El Tibio" Muñoz, an Olympic medal winner with no experience as a newscaster. The two of them felt so awkward in front of the cameras that they drank coffee on the air to distract the viewers from their clumsiness. KMEX was affiliated with the Spanish International Network (SIN), which later became *Univisión*. Early one morning, two executives from SIN who were visiting L.A. caught their morning show, then contacted Jorge to offer him a job as co-host of *Mundo Latino* (Latino World), a morning variety show based in Miami that required him to report news, cook food and dance salsa on the air.

---

145 "10 Questions for Jorge Ramos."

Just months after moving to Florida, a crisis at SIN created an opening in the evening news, a position which Jorge was eager to fill. At the age of 28, he became one of the youngest national news anchors in the history of television. He was so green that he didn't know how to use the teleprompter properly and he needed help keeping his place. María Elena Salinas, who soon took over as his co-host, said that her first impressions of him gave no indication of the towering figure he would become. "I remember a skinny guy, kind of short," she said. "He didn't look like a powerful man. He looked very innocent. But when he started reporting, you began to see this warrior come out in him."[146] He looked so young that the make-up artist decided to dye his hair grey at the temples to provide an illusion of gravitas.

In his autobiography *No Borders*, Jorge expresses his frank admiration for his co-host María Elena Salinas, the daughter of Mexican immigrants who has fought hard to get ahead and help her family. She has juggled the roles of journalist, mother, friend, housekeeper, wife, and role model for young Latinas and, according to Jorge, she's not a "superwoman," but she's the closest to one that he has ever known. Jorge also gives much credit to Patsy Loris, who has worked behind the scenes, setting up interviews and opportunities for him to cover major events. Without her and the rest of the *Univisión* team, Jorge claims, his career would have gone up in smoke in an instant.

Jorge faced a somewhat hostile environment in Miami since the majority of the Spanish-speaking population consisted of Cubans, many of whom did not appreciate Mexico's close relations with Fidel Castro. Some Cubans said in person and on the radio that they would never accept Mexicans in general and Jorge in particular. Gradually, he made friends and influenced enemies, and the naysayers became the minority. With a baby face, zero credibility and a churning stomach, Jorge learned to assert himself and

146 Guthrie 2/2.

handle the pressure of appearing on live television while trying to explain extremely complex political situations in Latin America. He paid his own airfare and used vacation time in order to cover wars that his station thought were not of interest to their audience. A phone call in the middle of the night would send him off to any place in the world where there were natural catastrophes, historic events, breaking news, or important people to interview.

He has interviewed every U.S. president since George H.W. Bush, countless candidates, and almost every Latin American president in the last two decades. He flew in a plane that filled with smoke and almost crashed, hid in a hut in El Salvador while bullets rained down on the metal roof, walked through mine fields in Afghanistan, received death threats in Colombia, and visited a refugee camp in Kosovo where he saw his own children's eyes in the faces of the youngsters who were suffering from hunger, wounds, and abandonment.

Jorge has written extensively about all these experiences and many more in *No Borders* and *Lo que vi* (What I Saw), providing a personal, heartfelt account of the human toll of disasters caused by nature and people. After each event, he came back to Miami to pick up the pieces and pull himself together again. His return from Afghanistan was one of the roughest: after several months he was able to regain some mental balance, but the experience continued to haunt him for a long time. "But I still haven't been able to shake off that feeling of vulnerability I acquired in Afghanistan," he wrote, "and that made me see life as though it were a piece of glass ready to shatter."[147]

While working at *Univisión*, Jorge completed a Master's Degree in International Relations at the University of Miami. He has expressed interest in participating in politics, and that is an ambition that he has not discounted, but so far the main benefit

---

147 *No Borders* 208.

of this degree has been to increase his awareness of the context of the news he is reporting.

One of Jorge's strong points is his empathy. His senses are permeated with the affliction of others. The eyes of a flood victim who lost her children to the raging waters are seared into his own vision; the acrid smell of human ash, dust, and despair at the former World Trade Center after 9/11 continued to saturate his nostrils for days, the only odor that his reconstructed nose could perceive. The dead-turned-to-dust surrounded him at ground zero, and he was not able to escape their painful embrace as it constricted his chest. Whenever he reports on children who have suffered abuse or the ravages of war, he is thinking about how horrible it would be for his own children to endure such experiences.

Partly because he speaks from the heart, even while maintaining his professional anchorman face, Jorge is now the most popular Latino journalist in the United States and perhaps in all of Latin America. His phenomenal success as a news reporter and writer has been explained by Ricardo Brown, a host on *Radio Unica*, a national radio network: "People perceive him not only as a solid, honest, hard-working journalist, but as a warm, kind human being who identifies with the reality [of immigrants] here. All the success he's had is due to the same work ethic and desire to better your life that Hispanics here have. That's his magic."[148]

## A new breed of journalist: impartiality vs. advocacy

Jorge considers it his duty as an interviewer to challenge those in power to tell the truth, and to report that information to the public. According to University of Rochester Professor Beth Jörgensen, "He firmly holds that the successful working of democracy requires an active and fearless press that takes seriously its obligation to

148 Martin 3/7.

tell the truth..., but Ramos tends to emphasize that the most critical task of the journalist is not simply to inform but to serve as a counterbalance to those who hold power."[149] Jörgensen explains that his focus on exposing the shortcomings of politicians and denouncing social ills has not obscured "his underlying admiration and his fundamental desire to promote positive change."[150]

Columbia Professor Mirta Ojito wrote that "Ramos' lack of objectivity on immigration doesn't make him a bad journalist, but a different breed of journalist."[151] On screen, Jorge usually tries to keep a straight face and maintain the appearance of impartiality, even when he is overwhelmed with emotions about a particular event. In Mexico City when 71 years of domination by one party were ended by the election of the year 2000, Jorge wanted to scream with joy, but he had to control himself long enough to report the news. "He was so thrilled for his country that he could barely contain himself," according to Lydia Martin; however, "Ramos managed to cover all the hoopla and all the politics with his usual stiff upper lip....You would have had to know Ramos well to notice the happy crinkle around his ice-blue eyes."[152]

Jorge appears to maintain impartiality relatively well in regard to specific *politicians and parties*, both on television and in his writing, but he is an ardent advocate of certain *causes*, especially immigration reform and democracy in Latin America, as well as the rights of women, minorities, gays, and victims of sexual abuse. While reporting the news, he strives to maintain objectivity and present both sides of the story, as most journalists do, but in his written works and his political talk show, he expresses his opinions more openly.

---

149 Jörgensen 280.
150 Ibid. 282.
151 Costantini 1/1.
152 Martin 1/7.

On his *Al Punto* program of June 11, 2012, when he objected to the use of his image in a political ad produced by President Obama's re-election campaign, Jorge emphasized that he doesn't want to be dragged into partisan politics. He prefers to have the freedom to pressure both parties to work toward immigration reform and other reforms, and influence his viewers to support whichever side offers the most comprehensive and compassionate solution. This is often the Democrats' side, as he has acknowledged, but in an open letter to the Democrats published August 27, 2012, he warns them that Latinos will not wait forever for them to keep their promises. In an interview with Jorge during his 2008 presidential campaign, Obama had promised to send a significant proposal for immigration reform to Congress during his first year in office. Jorge recognizes that the president's decision in 2012 to halt deportations of undocumented students was an important step, but he believes that it hardly counts as immigration reform. "Promises are no longer enough," he states. "We want to be part of the process, and we want to be heard."[153]

In March of 2012, he published an article in *Time*, entitled "Why Neither Party Speaks Our Language Yet," in which he laments both the Democrats' broken promises and the Republicans' emphasis on securing the border while rejecting multiple immigration-reform proposals. Besides advocating for immigration reform, Jorge is known for presenting other stories of particular concern to Latinos. According to Joe Uva, CEO of *Univisión*, Jorge has become the voice of the Latino community. "He's so compelling," Joe says, "because he's so committed to making sure that issues that are of great importance to Hispanics in this country are accurately told and presented."[154]

---

153 "No Love Lost: An Open Letter to the Democrats" 2/2.
154 Guthrie 2/2.

## Voice of the immigrants

Jorge has been called the "voice of the voiceless," a term that perhaps has been overused, but is nonetheless appropriate.[155] In the preface of *A Country for All*, Jorge explains, "My goal in writing this book is to make the invisible visible, and to give voice to the voiceless." Jorge has written four books and countless articles about the situation of undocumented immigrants in this country, and even though he admits that on this subject he's an "organillero" (an organ grinder, i.e. a broken record), he finds numerous ways to make the topic fresh with personal stories, historic references, legal arguments, and numerous statistics that are updated each time he writes.

Although he does not deal directly with the philosophical problem of his role as an intellectual speaking for others who have been less privileged,[156] he has had to overcome many of the same obstacles as other immigrants, and he states that his goal is to have all immigrants treated as well as he has been treated. Moreover, he makes a concerted effort to allow others to speak for themselves whenever possible, by quoting them verbatim, publishing some of their letters, and describing their circumstances with sensitivity and attention to affective details. He praises the immigrants' perseverance and courage, calling them "true heroes,"[157] while criticizing a system that does not distinguish between hard-working family members and criminals. Immigrants endure extreme working conditions, constant fear of authorities, and protracted poverty in order to provide a better life for their children. "And that is exactly why," writes Jorge, "even though

155 For example, Elena Poniatowska has been called the voice of the voiceless for decades.
156 As pointed out by Jörgensen, 282.
157 "The Anchor" 2/3.

many Americans don't know that they exist, these immigrants are the strongest, bravest, most innovative, most persistent, most courageous, most devoted individuals you will ever meet."[158]

Jorge criticizes the labyrinth of arbitrary laws that only lawyers can interpret because the rules apply to different groups of people at different times and in different ways. Immigration specialists often take advantage of their clients, and petitioners have been arrested while presenting their papers at the INS, which has contributed to an atmosphere of confusion and fear.[159] The solution that Jorge proposes is a general amnesty —similar to the one in 1986— for undocumented immigrants, a path toward citizenship and toward complete integration into U.S. society, an uncomplicated legal pathway for new workers coming into the country, and a long-term investment in a plan to help Latin American nations shore up their economies and create better-paid jobs in their countries.[160] "Truly great nations are measured by the way they treat their most vulnerable residents," he declares in one of his columns.[161] Some of the other compelling reasons he offers for this reform are that immigrants bring in more benefits than they receive in services, and legalization would increase that amount; there is less crime and less poverty in areas with higher concentrations of immigrants; and more workers are needed to replace the retiring boomers.[162]

In *The Other Face of America*, Jorge tells numerous stories about immigrants from Mexico, Cuba, Puerto Rico, Central America and South America, describing their different circumstances and reasons for leaving their countries. He allows many of his interviewees to relate the highlights of their own stories, and

---

158 *A Country for All* 6.
159 *La otra cara de América* 243-245.
160 Ibid. 126.
161 "So Much for the Mexican Invasion" 2/2.
162 *A Country for All* 39-86.

includes two letters written by an undocumented immigrant and one by a Mexican girl who gave up on the American Dream and went back to her homeland. In *Dying to Cross*, Jorge tells the tragic story of the nineteen immigrants who died in an abandoned trailer in Victoria, Texas, based on interviews with some of the fifty-four survivors.

The autobiographical *No Borders* is an intimate, nostalgic portrayal of the first two decades of his life as an immigrant. "I have yet to find a place where I belong, either tangible or emotional," he explains. "I have lived in the United States for almost twenty years, and I still feel like an immigrant. In fact, if one day I decided to make the United States my permanent residence, I suspect that I would die feeling like an immigrant. It's an idea that makes me shudder."[163] During this period, when he returns to Mexico he does not feel at home anymore. He uses words from the Argentine singer Facundo Cabral's song, *"No soy de aquí, no soy de allá,"* (I'm not from here, I'm not from there) to explain his feeling of not fitting in anywhere. However, his philosophy seems to have evolved throughout the years. Even the translation of the title of his book reflects an affective and cognitive progression: *Atravesando fronteras* could be translated literally as "crossing borders," but it has been rendered as *No Borders*, a reflection of Jorge's current opinion that borders should be more fluent and permeable. Ironically, this concept brings him closer to a deeper meaning of Facundo Cabral's song, which is about being a citizen of the world rather than residing within geographic boundaries.[164]

A notable change in his attitude can be found in his more recent work, *The Gift of Time*, in which he reveals a lesson he learned from the Chilean author and immigrant Isabel Allende: "I am from two countries. And I can be. I don't have to choose."[165]

163 *No Borders* 1.
164 As interpreted by the singer himself in 1972.
165 *The Gift of Time* 99.

Jorge might be referring to the 1995 change in Mexican law that allows immigrants to maintain both Mexican and U.S. citizenship, but there is more to it than that. It's about cultural hybridity or multiculturalism, a mixing or peaceful coexistence of cultures within an individual or within a society. "[The United States] is becoming so Latin Americanized," he explains, "that I'm constantly feeling more and more at home, and the rest of Latin America is becoming Americanized. And I'm sitting right in the middle, between the two parent nations. I'm always home."[166]

Jorge uses his own story and that of thousands of other immigrants in order to provide faces for the invisible immigrants in our country. He makes the legal argument that the Constitution does not specify that the rights to justice, welfare and liberty only apply to those who carry U.S. passports or green cards, but rather they should apply to everyone within our borders. To push for successful reforms, he proposes what he calls "Project 279" because 279 people have to be convinced of the need for real change: 218 representatives, 60 senators, and the president.[167]

According to Jorge, we all benefit from the labor of undocumented workers. They provide child care, clean houses, pick fruits and vegetables, and work in stores, restaurants and hotels; they also construct buildings, roads, and other infrastructure. In order to avoid any contact with undocumented immigrants or the fruit of their labors, one would have to live on Mars. Thus we are all complicit in the plight of the undocumented workers.[168] This concept is humorously addressed in the movie "A Day Without a Mexican," in which Californians are stunned when the wheels of everyday life grind to a halt without the contributions of countless Mexicans who suddenly disappear.

---

166 Ibid. 109.

167 This paragraph summarizes information in *A Country for All* 36 - 81.

168 *La otra cara de América* 237-239.

In 2013, as support for immigration reform increased in spite of a series of roadblocks thrown up by the opposition, Jorge churned out a series of columns about the issue. He obviously will not rest until a comprehensive, inclusive reform is passed and implemented.

## Advocate for Peace, Democracy and Rights for all

Jorge takes advocative journalism to a new level in the moving, heartfelt collection of letters to his children, *The Gift of Time*. In one letter, he describes himself as a "humanitarian journalist" and tries to convey the violence, fear, desperation and isolation of war. His words are particularly valuable because of his experiences covering five wars: El Salvador, Kosovo, the Persian Gulf, Afghanistan, and Iraq. "War is failure," he writes. "War is the absolute confirmation that we fail as human beings, that we cannot converse with one another, that we aren't as ready as we think we are, that we haven't learned from the fighting –and the dying—that came before us."[169] According to Jorge, a soldier is only able to kill because he is cut off from his humanity:

> Kill or be killed. The person standing in front of you is not a father, not a son, not a friend of anybody. War strips you of your environment because –if it doesn't— you can't kill. How could you shoot someone if you're worried about whether he has any children? How can you kill a young man if you're thinking about the grief of his parents?
>
> Nothing is more dangerous than dividing the world into black and white, into good and evil. Rulers who think in such terms are like cowboys in a power struggle. Even the dumbest of them feel superior to others. And

---

169 *The Gift of Time* 36.

that always results in confrontation. [170]

In broad, optimistic terms that reflect his multicultural perspective, Jorge suggests a path to peace: "[We need to] find some sort of structure under which we can live peacefully with extremely different cultures and ideologies. We need an international order that fosters contact among contrary systems of beliefs and eliminates the desire to destroy."[171]

Jorge has felt the effects of war on his psyche, since his experiences were so extreme that his body closed off from the exterior world as a means of self-protection. In his letters to his children he makes an attempt to chip away the shield that hides his emotions: "I feel like a sculptor chiseling away, piece by piece, at a mask that took years to set into place."[172]

Mexico's faltering democracy is another cause that evokes powerful emotions in Jorge. He rejoiced at the presidential election in the year 2000 that ended a 71-year domination by the PRI (the official party), but he was crushed in 2012 when the PRI regained the presidency in a campaign that was plagued by fraud. In an article published shortly after the election, Jorge states that the PRI may have influenced the results by buying the votes of thousands, or even millions, of Mexicans; he challenges Mexicans to break the habit of passive acceptance, and stand together to prevent this from ever happening again.[173]

Jorge often calls on journalists to denounce abuses of power in Mexico and in all of Latin America, as well as in the United States. In his autobiography, he explains that in Latin America, journalists compensate for the lack of institutionalized justice, fulfilling duties that should be carried out by police, prosecutors and

170 Ibid. 36-37.
171 Ibid. 108.
172 Ibid. 49.
173 "For Mexicans, It's Time to Take Sides" 1/2.

official defenders of human rights.[174] He explains that poverty and regimes based on charismatic leaders rather than institutions are the principal threats to progress in Latin America. Where laws are not respected, corruption reigns, and the United States has been too preoccupied with protecting its own interests to help make qualitative changes in the area.[175]

Jorge's causes are not limited to those who are similar to him; rather, he finds common ground with a wide variety of people who have experienced injustice. He calls himself an ardent defender of feminism, and despite his seemingly problematic relationship with significant others, he has given credit to several women for inspiring and helping him with his career, and he has spoken out against the inequalities that he perceives in society. In one of his columns, he denounced the Catholic Church for its archaic policies toward women, particularly for not allowing women to be priests. "This is simply discrimination," he declares, "and by a church that preaches equality and therefore should not treat half the population as inferior."[176] In "The Vatican's New Habit: Attacking Nuns," he came to the defense of Sister Margaret Farley, whose book *Just Love: A Framework for Christian Sexual Ethics* was condemned by the Vatican for demanding change regarding the church's inflexible notions of sexual morality. Perhaps it was Farley's defense of female masturbation that riled the church's censors the most, but according to Jorge, "the real problem is that [she is] questioning the Catholic Church's structure, which was founded on the assertion that only men should be in power and make decisions, that only men can judge what is or is not moral."[177]

In the conclusion of the abovementioned article, Jorge states that the Vatican's main problem is men, not women, a theme that

---

174 *Atravesando fronteras* 268.
175 Ibid. 227-268.
176 "Of Popes and Prophylactics" 2/2.
177 "The Vatican's New Habit" 2/2.

he returns to in his column "Fighting 'Monsters in Clerical Garb',"
which is a passionate condemnation of the abuses by pedophile
priests and the cover-up of those abuses. He references his
own experience of being beaten by priests at his private school,
expressing outrage at the fact that nobody said or did anything
to defend him and the other children being beaten on a regular
basis. He encourages people to speak out against sexual abuse and
physical beatings alike, and "tell the monsters in clerical garb, and
their accomplices, that they no longer have free rein to terrorize
the innocent."[178]

Another cause that Jorge has championed is gay rights. As the
moderator of a debate on gay rights, he tried to maintain objectivity,
but when the speaker who opposed gay rights repeatedly avoided
answering his incisive questions, Jorge pointed out that it was
a matter of equality, and in the United States one should not
discriminate against anybody.[179] In an article published in May
2012, "A Step Forward for Gay Rights," Jorge applauds Obama's
announcement that he supports gay marriage. In his April 2013
column, "Let Them Tie the Knot," he advocates for the legalization
of same-sex marriage at the national level.

Occasionally, Jorge will reveal his sense of humor as an interest-
grabbing technique. In "Of Popes and Prophylactics," he criticizes
the Catholic Church's opposition to the use of birth control, catching
the reader's attention with this hilarious opening statement: "I
have never known anyone who, in the heat of the moment, has
suddenly stopped unwrapping a condom to ponder what Pope
Benedict XVI would have to say about it. Not one." Then he changes
his tone dramatically: "But to forbid the use of condoms in the age
of AIDS is basically to sentence millions to death. It is that simple.
It is that urgent."[180] Obviously, the use of condoms would be only a

178 "Fighting 'Monsters in Clerical Garb'" 2/2.
179 *Al Punto*, May 14, 2012.
180 "Of Popes and Prophylactics" 1/2.

partial solution to the global AIDS pandemic, but Jorge's point was that thousands of lives could be saved if religious leaders would advise people to use condoms.

## Jorge's books

Jorge loves to read, and considers some books to be akin to best friends. In his letters to his children, he makes numerous references to great works of literature, which he credits for shaping his life: "Time is a constant theme throughout literature, but it was literature itself that helped me understand the nature of time, and —by extension—life itself. The things I found in books changed the way in which I perceived things in real life."[181]

The books Jorge has written are all nonfiction and often testimonial. He writes in a clear, journalistic style that is accessible to the wide audience he is trying to reach. The translations are well done, and appropriate to his style and audience. He has written four books on the issue of immigration: *The Other Face of America, Dying to Cross, The Latino Wave,* and *A Country for All*, as well as his autobiography *No Borders*, which tells his own story of immigrating to the United States and finding success here. He has published three collections of his interviews with some of the most powerful people in Latin America: *Detrás de la máscara* (Behind the mask); *A la caza del león* (Hunting the lion); and *Los presidenciables* (The presidential contenders), which have not been translated. The latter work includes conversations with the top 6 candidates in Mexico's 2012 election, the winner of the 2006 election, and several former presidents. In this work he establishes the historical and political context for the interviews, and makes a determined plea for Mexicans to continue striving toward a true democracy. In his early work, *Lo que vi* (What I saw),

---

181 *The Gift of Time* 145.

he shares some of the extraordinary experiences he has had as a broadcast journalist. *The Gift of Time: Letters from a Father* seems to be a sincere attempt to communicate with his children, while offering insights and advice to all those who may have something in common with him. Lastly, his children's book *I'm Just Like My Mom/I'm Just Like My Dad* is a delightful celebration of what parents and children share.

For a few years beginning in 2002, Jorge hosted a literary talk show that he created, *Despierta Leyendo*, (Wake up by Reading), during which he would recommend three books –fiction, nonfiction, and children's—which often became bestsellers after being discussed on his show.

Jorge has been recognized for his promotion of literature and education. He won the Ruben Salazar Award by the National Council of La Raza for his positive portrayal of Latinos in 2002, and the Latino Book Award of 2006 for *Dying to Cross*. The American Association of Publishers' Honors Award was bestowed upon him in 2004, and that same year he earned the Cervantes Award of Dade County for "the most significant contribution to the enhancement of Hispanic education." The University of Richmond recognized him with an honorary doctorate in literature in 2007.[182] In 2010, Jorge donated $20,000 worth of scholarships for undocumented immigrants who want to study at universities in the United States, and he has encouraged others to make contributions to this cause. The scholarships are administered by the Educators for Fair Consideration (E4FC).[183]

---

182 For details about these and other awards, see "Jorge Ramos Biography."
183 "Jorge Ramos ayuda con becas a inmigrantes indocumentados."

## Fatherhood

Of all his writings, *The Gift of Time: Letters from a Father* is the work that most clearly states his priorities in life: first his children, then his job. He wrote these letters to fill in the gaps in his relationships with his son and daughter, Nicolás and Paola. He was motivated by a close call on the freeway when he was almost hit head-on by a speeding van, which gave him such a scare that he realized he needed to write something to leave his children in case he's not so lucky the next time. The irony of almost being wiped out as he was driving to the dentist on a sunny Florida morning, after all the times he escaped death during wars and other catastrophes, was not lost on him. He regrets that he did not get to know his own father very well, and he wants his children to know him and to learn from him.

Although he reconciled with his father after having left home, the conflict and lack of communication with his dad left an indelible mark on Jorge's character. In fact, as far as I know, the only time that tears came to his eyes while on television was on Cristina Saralegui's *Show de Cristina*, when he was talking about his father. Jorge learned by opposing his father. He perceived his father as being unhappy in his work as an architect, so Jorge decided to do the opposite of what his father did, and thus chose a career that he cared about passionately. And that is the most important piece of advice that he has for his children: do what you love, even if it's not a sure path to society's approval or financial success. "To advance, you have to rebel," he explains. "And sometimes the hardest thing to do is to rebel against the comfort and mediocrity of our own lives."[184]

When he's not busy giving them advice, Jorge admits to learning

---

184 *The Gift of Time* 142.

a lot from his children, who are more comfortable speaking English than Spanish. The fact that they do not watch his news programs is one of the factors motivating him to collaborate on the creation of the new network for Latinos who prefer to watch programs in English.

Jorge laments that the demands of his profession have often separated him from his children, and he expresses profound pain at not being able to spend as much time with them as he wishes. When describing how he had to rush to ground zero on 9/11 instead of hurrying home to comfort his loved ones, he confesses: "Something breaks inside of you when your heart begs to be with your children and yet, for some reason, you cannot."[185]

## Secrets of his success

The advice he offers his children provides some clues to the secrets of his success. He recommends identifying your fears and figuring out how to overcome them, and he quotes Ralph Waldo Emerson: "He who is not every day conquering some fear has not learned the secret of life."[186] Jorge admits that he has felt afraid in many situations, but he has persevered despite his fears. He does not believe in destiny nor in a divine plan, but rather that you have to make your own plan and carry it through. He urges his children to keep learning, trying new things, and traveling to as many places as possible. While in a new country, he tells them, you should participate in local life as much as possible and not be judgmental. You need to be persistent in pursuing your goals, be independent, be leaders rather than followers, and be transcendent, going beyond yourselves to make the world a better place. Use money to give you more freedom when making

185 Ibid. 97.
186 Ibid. 89.

decisions, and not necessarily for material possessions, which will hinder you and drag you down. Above all, define your own identity, and live life with passion, he counsels.[187]

A vital piece of advice which explains his advocacy of so many causes is that it is important to take sides. One should not hesitate to denounce an injustice or to confront people in power who are abusing their positions. Jorge quotes a survivor of a Nazi concentration camp, Elie Wiesel, who said, "Neutrality helps the oppressor, never the victim."[188] Jorge tells his children that sometimes it is not easy to speak out, but life is too short to walk around being neutral. I believe that Jorge's willingness to take a stand and his ability to overcome his fears are two very important keys to his success. His sense of humor, gratitude toward others, love of adventure and eagerness for new challenges have all contributed to his progress along the way.

### A life in perspective

As a public figure who figures prominently in the mass media, Jorge has received more than his share of criticism. He has been accused of speaking for the underdogs from a position of privilege, of being a cultural separatist (speaking only for Latinos), and of promoting conservative Latino values that might limit other people's freedoms, such as opposition to divorce, gender equity, and homosexuality. It seems that such accusations come from people who do not know his personal story and have not read much of what he has written. In regard to the first accusation, Jorge has dealt with the issue of speaking for others by showing empathy and allowing his interviewees to speak for themselves. Second, he

---

187 This paragraph is a summary and paraphrase of advice given in *The Gift of Time* 89-185.
188 *The Gift of Time* 179.

transcends cultural separatism by affirming his double, or even global identity. He accepts the many currents flowing within him, and has achieved a measure of harmony: "I fit perfectly into a multiethnic, multicultural, multiracial, and multilingual society.... The United States is a unique place where foreigners cease to be foreign."[189] And third, in regard to values that restrict others' freedoms, he has mentioned that some Latinos have conservative values that align with the Republican Party's platform, but he has not advocated for those values. In fact, he has rebelled against restrictions on his own freedom, and his advocacy of women's rights and gay rights is well documented. "I want a healthier planet," he tells his children. "Less crime. Less hunger. I want men and women to be equals on the street, in the office, in the churches, and in the schools."[190] However, if Jorge has an Achilles' heel, it is probably in regard to his romantic relationships with women. He has dealt with the criticism he has received because of this issue by accepting responsibility for the failure of his marriages. In his published letters to his children, he affirmed his commitment to them and expressed regret for all of the times he has had to leave them in order to pursue a story.

Another issue to consider is the dynamic tension between Jorge's masking his emotions and expressing them, as well as between his remaining impartial and taking sides. Besides being a reaction to extreme experiences with war and disasters, the mask he wears seems to be the result of family dynamics and his reserved character. He has made a valiant attempt to open up, communicate with his children and others, and generally to have more fun rather than hide behind a serious façade. He has found a way to combine advocative journalism in writing and

189 Ibid. 99.
190 Ibid. 170.

on his talk show *Al Punto*, with objective reporting during his evening news show. And yet, he sometimes cannot hide his joy or disappointment with the news. As he signs off, there occasionally is a sparkle in his eyes or a slight grimace on his face. Thus Jorge reveals his humanity and, as Walter Cronkite used to do, he helps his viewers absorb the news and deal with the emotions that are provoked by joyous or tragic events.

Jorge has persevered all these years and created his own path to success by dealing with his fears, ignoring the naysayers and paying attention to inspirational people, such as his liberated mother, his story-telling grandfather, the courageous writer Elena Poniatowska, and the intrepid interviewer Oriana Fallaci. He pursued his goals with steadfast determination, and he chose those goals carefully. He gave up his dream of becoming a concert guitarist when he realized that he was better at expressing himself with words than with music. When a serious back problem prevented him from pursuing his Olympic ambitions, he absorbed that blow and used it as an opportunity to learn an important lesson: some dreams are not attainable, so you have to go after the ones that are.

Life has not always been easy for Jorge, who sometimes had to sell walnuts on the streets when he was a child. Later, he worked long hours at a series of jobs to help pay for his education, while commuting across one of the largest cities in the world and striving to maintain his grades. The obstacles that Jorge has overcome include being beaten repeatedly by priests at his school, being forced to quit his job at a Mexican radio station, and having to live with what he described as "crushing loneliness" after leaving everything and everybody behind when he immigrated to the United States. Even as a successful news anchor, he still has to override his inherent timidity every time he faces a camera. Thus, he has overcome adversity, worked hard to improve the lives of others, and served as a role model for young Latinos. He is reaching out to Latinos who cannot speak Spanish, and to non-Latinos also. As the English-language channel *Fusion* becomes better known, Jorge will be addressing an ever-expanding audience and greatly increasing the awareness of and sympathy for Latino issues.

Jorge frequently has expressed his deep gratitude for the freedom he enjoys in this country, particularly the freedom of expression. The epigraph of this chapter on Jorge is a quote from an article that he wrote on the thirtieth anniversary of his arrival in the United States. The larger font for the final words of his article, "Thank you, thank you, thank you," is Jorge's emphasis. Judging by all the contributions he has made to a wide variety of causes, he certainly has accepted the responsibility that comes with that freedom.

§ § §

## Works Cited

### Books

Ramos Avalos, Jorge. *A Country for All: An Immigrant Manifesto.* Trans. Ezra Fitz. New York: Random House, 2010. Spanish title: *Tierra de todos: Nuestro momento para crear una nación de iguales.* Random House, 2009.

---. *The Gift of Time: Letters from a Father.* Trans. Ezra Fitz. New York: HarperCollins, 2008. Spanish title: *El regalo del tiempo.* Harper Collins, 2007.

---. *Los presidenciables: Las entrevistas incómodas con los que quieren el poder y con los que ya lo tuvieron.* Mexico: Grijalbo, 2011.

---. *No Borders: A Journalist's Search for Home.* Trans. Patricia J. Duncan. New York: HarperCollins, 2002. Spanish title: *Atravesando fronteras: la autobiografía de un periodista en busca de su lugar en el mundo.* HarperCollins, 2002.

---. *The Other Face of America: Chronicles of the Immigrants Shaping Our Future.* New York: HarperCollins, 2002. Spanish title: *La otra cara de América: Historias de los inmigrantes latinoamericanos que están cambiando a Estados Unidos.* Mexico: Grijalbo, 2003 (first ed. 2000).

### Video, Articles and Web Pages (web pages accessed August-September, 2012)

"10 Questions for Jorge Ramos." *Time.* 09 Aug 2010. Vol. 176,

Issue 6, p. 6.

"A Day Without a Mexican." Film directed by Sergio Arau. 2004.

"Al Punto." Televised 14 May 2012.

"The Anchor." Jorge Ramos web site. http://jorgeramos.com. From *The Orange County Register*. Oct 2000.

"The Colbert Report." 2 Oct 2012. From Stephen Colbert's website: http://www.colbertnation.com.

Costantini, Cristina. "Jorge Ramos, Univision Anchor, Speaks Out on SP1070 Ruling, Navigates Journalistic Impartiality." Huffington Post web site. http://www.huffingtonpost.com/2012/06/27.

Guthrie, Marisa. "Jorge Ramos." *Broadcasting & Cable*. 19 Oct 2009: 16. *Academic OneFile*.

"Jaime Bayly entrevista a Jorge Ramos." 5 Aug 2008. Daniperu 25. http://www.youtube.com.

"Jorge Ramos ayuda con becas a inmigrantes indocumentados." Huffington Post website. http://noticias.aollatino.com/2010/11/22.

"Jorge Ramos Biography." Jorge Ramos web site. http://jorgeramos.com.

Jörgensen, Beth. "Jorge Ramos Reads North from South." *Mexico Reading the United States*. Ed. Linda Egan and Mary K. Long. Nashville: Vanderbilt University Press, 2009.

Martin, Lydia. "Jorge Ramos Making News." *Hispanic*. Jan/Feb 2001, Vol 14, Issue 1/2: 62. *Academic Search Premier*.

Martínez, Laura. "Making News: Univision's Jorge Ramos Receives Lifetime Achievement Award." Multichannel News web site. 18 Oct 2008. http://www.multichannel.com.

Ramos Avalos, Jorge. "Fighting 'Monsters in Clerical Garb'." Jorge Ramos web site. 03 Aug 2012. http://jorgeramos.com.

---. "For Mexicans It's Time to Take Sides." Jorge Ramos web site. 18 Jul 2012. http://jorgeramos.com.

---. "No Love Lost: An Open Letter to the Democrats." Jorge Ramos web site. 27 Aug 2012. http://jorgeramos.com.

---. "Of Popes and Prophylactics." Jorge Ramos web site. 11 Oct 2010. http://jorgeramos.com.

---. "So Much for the Mexican Invasion." Jorge Ramos web site. 30 Apr 2012. http://jorgeramos.com.

---. "The Vatican's New Habit: Attacking Nuns." Jorge Ramos web site. 11 Jun 2012. http://jorgeramos.com.

---. "Why Neither Party Speaks Our Language Yet." *Time*. 5 Mar 2012.

Roig-Franzia, Manuel and Peter Wallsten. "A new audience, en Inglés, por favor." *The Washington Post*. 19 Feb 2013.

# John Haroldson and María Chávez-Haroldson

The Haroldsons in front of courthouse

María Chávez-Haroldson.   John reads in Spanish at elementary school

Investigating a case. --Photo by Jesse Skoubo, Corvallis Gazette-Times

118

## Chapter Four

## John Haroldson and María Teresa Chávez-Haroldson:

## District Attorney and Leadership Facilitator

"Keep moving forward no matter what,
one foot in front of the other."

--María Chávez-Haroldson

As dual citizens of Mexico and the United States, John Haroldson and María Teresa Chávez-Haroldson are an impressive team. As children of immigrants, they both have experienced discrimination, poverty, extremely challenging work, frequent moves, and a struggle to establish personal identity while straddling two cultures in a sometimes hostile environment. When they got married nine years ago, they became a strong force on the side of social and legal justice.[191] These two people, while operating primarily on the local level, have also had some impact on the state, national and international levels.

The Haroldsons are a striking couple. John has a tall, slender frame, dark hair and eyes, and a fair complexion; he carries himself with a correctness and dignity that belie the struggles and

---

191 Most of the information for this chapter comes from unpublished oral and written interviews and materials provided to me by the Haroldsons from November 2012 to January 2013. If a source is not identified, that indicates that the source is one of these interviews. Once again I ask for the reader's understanding about my use of John and María's first names. I have chosen to use their first names because I am writing about their personal stories as well as their careers, and I wish to help the reader identify with them.

health crises he has faced. María has golden brown skin, wavy hair, and a lovely face that conveys her inner strength. Although they are physically attractive, the Haroldsons are far from being typical "beautiful people," since they both have dedicated their energy and resources to improving the lives of other individuals and communities.

After a childhood during which he often had to fight numerous classmates who ostracized him and taunted him with racial epithets, John decided to go to law school and eventually to become a district attorney so that he could have a seat at the table of justice; thus, instead of being defined by his anger, he could work for positive change. Starting at a young age, María Teresa first helped care for her nine siblings, then raised her own four children without much help. She now has six grandchildren, who all live nearby. While single-parenting and working full time, she went back to school for an undergraduate degree, and in June 2013 she completed her master's degree and was accepted into a doctoral program in Leadership and Change. A victim of violent crime herself, she became the first Latina to be director of the Crime Victim's Unit in Yamhill County, Oregon, and she is currently the associate director of the Center for Latin@ Studies and Engagement at Oregon State University.

During what John and María call their "free time," they have worked together to conduct mock trials for Latino students, given presentations on leadership and other important issues for numerous Hispanic organizations, presented on judicial reform and victims' rights in Mexico and Guatemala, and organized Oregon delegations to regional and national conferences of the United States Hispanic Leadership Institute. In 2013, John was elected vice chairman of the Oregon Commission on Hispanic Affairs, an eleven-member council that works to promote economic, social, political and legal equality for Latinos living in Oregon.

María Teresa and John have defied overwhelming odds and obtained success for themselves while helping many others to survive and succeed as well. They have done so by adhering to a vigorous work routine and persevering under extreme conditions, but there is something more to their story. When these two people talk about each other, their synergy electrifies the air. María insists that John has given her wings and has made her dream a reality. She admires his dedication to making the legal system equitable and accessible, and she is pleased to have a partner in her struggle for social justice. John gives María credit for his being able to survive two serious diseases: juvenile diabetes and diffuse scleroderma, which is a connective tissue disease affecting the skin, blood vessels, muscles, and internal organs. The average mortality rate for diffuse scleroderma is five years, but John has survived for fifteen years so far, and he intends to keep on kicking as long as he can: "¡hasta que me entierren! (until they bury me)," he exclaims. John calls María "his inspiration," and he speaks fondly of her beauty and grace. "When María dances," he remarks, "there is nothing that is remembered, it just flows, it happens; it's literally like watching someone who is a natural runner run, and it's a beautiful thing to see." María has taught John to dance, and she has proven to be such a skillful instructor that they have been able to lead a salsa dance class together. They enjoy singing together, and they performed in a community theater play, "*Bocón*," (Blabber-mouth) in February 2013, during which they sang a song that María's mother used to sing to her. The play tells the story of a twelve-year-old boy who flees a repressive regime in Central America and finds his way to the United States. The Haroldsons played the parents of the young immigrant, and thus they represented the heritage that immigrants carry with them on their journey and continue to cherish while residing in this country.

John and María's personal and professional lives are so intertwined that it seems appropriate to tell their stories in a single chapter rather than in two separate chapters.

## Early years: poverty and wealth

As children, both John and María lived through the hardships that are commonly faced by immigrants in the United States. John's father was the son of a Norwegian immigrant, and his mother was the thirteenth child in a very poor Mexican family. The two of them met in Monterrey, when John's father was visiting Mexico with some friends. John's parents began their married life in the state of Washington, where John was born in 1962. The family soon moved back to Mexico, so John spent the first four years of his life there, and Spanish became his first language. When his family returned to the U.S., attending school became a challenge because at that time there were no bilingual or English as a Second Language programs. His ability to speak Spanish was treated more like a learning disability than as a skill to be valued and developed. What made matters worse was that John's family moved around a lot, so he was always the new kid in school and usually he and his family were the only Latinos in the community. They lived in eight different cities in Washington and spent one year in Idaho. His strong desire to belong was usually thwarted, and he began to feel a certain detachment and isolation.

As a young adult he saw Sylvester Stallone in *First Blood* and identified with the hero who persevered against all odds despite being grossly outnumbered. When he was in the eighth grade, John was playing football with a group of children about his age and one of the players called him a spic. He had to fight with that child, and then another one called him a spic and he had to fight again. That happened repeatedly until he grew tired and admitted to himself, "I can't make this stop." It was then that he resolved to get an education so that he could be in a position to do something about racial discrimination.

A similar theme of defying the odds runs through María Teresa's childhood. She was the oldest daughter in a traditional Mexican family. She was born in Chihuahua, Mexico, in 1957. Her family immigrated to Manteca, California, and then moved to Azusa, California when María was in the third grade. Her mother was a homemaker with a fifth-grade education who had a deep love and dedication to her children. Maria's father was a machinist with a talent for music, which offered him opportunities to bring some extra income to his household. María sometimes faced blatant hostility in her community, as she illustrates with this anecdote:

> At a very young age (eight years old), I experienced something that I believe has led me to my community activism and crime victim advocacy as a professional. I was standing in line at a drug store during an era when smoking was allowed in businesses and stores. I had brought three younger siblings to the store to buy ice cream cones. In the store there was a very large man wearing cowboy boots (I kept looking down, so I only heard his voice and saw what appeared to be Paul Bunyan-sized boots). While we were standing in line, this huge man made some derogatory remarks about 'dirty Mexicans' and began to drop his cigarette ashes onto the top of my head. He did so for what seemed like a long time, long enough to feel the ashes burn my hair and scalp multiple times. I was afraid of him, so I only looked forward and did not say a word, since I was concentrating on protecting my siblings as they stood in line to buy their ice cream cones.

María remembers being given a white-skinned doll as a gift. She recalls that when she was a child, toys that reflected the realities of people of color were not available. Fortunately, she abandoned her doll on a heater, and when she came back later the doll had been toasted to a golden brown color and it looked like a little Mexican girl. She was thrilled that the doll looked more like her.

John grew up in poverty, and he remembers working in the fields and doing other hard labor for low wages in order to help make ends meet. He remembers digging potatoes, mixing concrete, and rubbing all the paint off a mobile home. "We were collectivists," John says. "We were a colony of ants, all working together for a common cause." He and his three brothers would work from morning to night, and their parents thought that was good for their work ethic. The four siblings once received a 100-pound bag of potatoes as payment for a couple of weeks of strenuous fieldwork that all four of them had done. John's father earned a master's degree and found work as a school teacher, but soon decided to go back to graduate school. John recalls living off lentils while his father worked on completing his doctorate. "But my father was an incredible role model," John explains, "he finished his Ph.D. in one year, and he gave me an example of how to give 100% when opportunities are there to make a change, and how to bring all the family together, because we all took paper routes and we found other ways to make money so that we as a family could continue to progress." John's father later became superintendent of schools in Hunters and then in Endicott, both in Washington state.

María's father also exemplified a strong work ethic, holding down two jobs in an effort to provide for his family. Nevertheless, María had to work hard to earn her own money to buy school clothes. Her first job was with a community-based tutoring program. During her early years as a married woman, some of her jobs included manual labor such as clearing logs, cleaning homes, clearing brush from fields, or picking produce.

A wealth of family traditions provides both contrast and counterbalance to economic hardship. "There were children who were raised in poverty," observes John, "who did not know that they were raised in poverty because of the human wealth that was part of their experience." This was true in María's family, since her father's second job was as a musician. "And here's the richness," she explains, "the cultural connection that he brought to all ten children through his music. He never learned how to read music, it was really a matter of the heart and soul." María describes the effect that music has had on her life:

> [My father] would transform our house on the weekends when he played his accordion or his piano or his organ...but what we came to recognize was the rhythm of life, because we would dance in the kitchen and it would bring some levity to whatever issues we were dealing with. Music got us through. And then the richness of the boleros —incredible songs of love and passion and forgiveness and never giving up, the richness of mother earth and your place of birth— it just filled the air throughout my life as I was growing up...We still get together and sing, and my children, who are not completely bilingual, will know the words to the songs because they've heard them so much. That's the incredible power of music.

María still dances in the kitchen as she cooks, and sings along to Latino music when she is driving alone in her car.

### Moving on (and up)

María's first language was Spanish and her parents did not speak English, so she struggled to keep up in school. Every day she helped care for her siblings and do household chores, and the prospect of college seemed like an impossible goal to her. She gave up on high school and married at a young age. Later, she earned her high school diploma by attending adult education classes. After her husband was injured on the job, they left southern California with their four children and moved to a place in the country near Brownsville, Oregon. When that marriage ended due to domestic violence she felt she was finally free to make her own decisions. Therefore, at the age of forty she chose to begin her college education, while continuing to work full-time and raise her two teenage daughters. Her other two children were adults and living on their own. When she applied for a job with the Crime Victim's Unit in Linn County, John Haroldson was on the interview panel, assigned to assess her fluency in Spanish. She passed with flying colors after having told a joke in Spanish, a task that had caused other candidates to panic.

At that time, John was working as the Linn County Deputy District Attorney, having completed internships as an Albany City Prosecutor and Lane County Public Defender. He had graduated from Central Washington University with a bachelor's degree in Philosophy and received his doctorate in Jurisprudence from the University of Oregon. After María Teresa accepted the job with the Crime Victim's Unit in Albany, she and John began to work together frequently, since they were assigned to the cases with Spanish-speaking victims. She would address the crime victim issues and provide court advocacy, and he was the assigned prosecutor since he was the only one in the D.A.'s office who spoke Spanish. They got to know each other professionally, but when María moved to New Mexico she and John lost touch for some time. Years later, María was working as the director of the Crime Victim's Unit for Yamhill County in McMinnville, Oregon. While unpacking a box of books that had been in storage, she came upon *The Mastery of Love* by Don Miguel Ruiz, a book that John had lent her. This gave her an excuse to go looking for John, and she knew that he was so disciplined that he would be at the Albany courthouse, even on a Saturday. She saw his car and went to his office window to throw some pebbles, since the courthouse was locked. He came out to greet her, and the relationship that ensued became much more than merely professional; four years later they were married.

## A dynamic duo

This is where their story really takes flight. In 2007, John became Oregon's first Mexican-American district attorney. Governor Ted Kulongoski appointed him to the position of Benton County District Attorney in order to replace a retiring prosecutor. A year later John was elected to the same position, and in 2012 he was re-elected, having been recognized for excellence in prosecution by the Oregon Crime Victims Assistance Network and the Oregon Humane Society.[192] María Teresa quit her job in McMinnville and moved with him to Corvallis, where she established a business called *Culturally Responsive Solutions*. In 2010 she became the executive director of Court Appointed Special Advocates-Voices for Children, and in 2012 she assumed her current position as associate director of the Center for Latin@ Studies and Engagement at Oregon State University (OSU). She has completed her master's degree in Public Administration, and has begun work on a Ph.D. in Leadership and Change through Antioch University in Seattle. She plans to focus on leadership as it relates to education, social justice, and Latino communities.

During his "spare time," John reads to children in Spanish at Garfield Elementary School, where he participated in the Start Making a Reader Today (SMART) program for several years. Since the program was canceled he has continued to read to students on his own. As a member of the advisory board for the César Chávez Cultural Center at OSU, he helps Latino students plan educational and social events at the university. He has been an adjunct faculty member at Willamette University School of Law, and currently is

---

192 *Oregon Voter's Guide*, 2012.

vice chair of the Oregon Commission of Hispanic Affairs. He serves on the Oregon State Bar Affirmative Action Committee and the Oregon State Bar Mentoring Task Force.[193] María has provided parenting classes to rural Latinos, and she has tried to empower Latina women by teaching them survival skills that they can pass on to others, thus creating a small army of Latinas. John and María have worked together on presentations for the College Assistance Migrant Program and the Oregon Migrant Leadership Institute. As part of the Oregon 4-H Youth Development Program, their mock-trial exercises for Latinos from grade school through high school have given Latino youths the opportunity to play the part of judge, prosecutor or defense attorney, and to imagine themselves in these real-life roles. Many of the participants have had life-changing experiences and have been inspired to become lawyers. As an example of their pedagogical strategy, John mentions a child who was not proficient in English and therefore was picked on, even among the Latinos. John chose him to be the prosecutor so that he could be in a position of power, and they held the trial in Spanish, which allowed the child to demonstrate his speaking skills and thus improve his status with the other children. The Haroldsons' philosophy is "to view the child as bringing a vessel full of cultural knowledge to the table, rather than bringing a vacant vessel or a deficit to the table."

John has been reading to elementary school children for a number of years now, and he has enjoyed watching some of them progress into the 4-H programs, as well as following some of the 4-H participants who continue on to Ivy League universities. "It's been an incredible journey for them, and it's been wonderful to be able to watch and support that process," says John. "I call that culturally responsive, relationship-based, wrap-around services for student leaders. And that's not coming from an educational

---

193 Oregon Commission on Hispanic Affairs, 2011 Annual Report, p. 11.

institution, but from the community."

Mario A. Magaña, the 4-H Outreach Specialist at Oregon State University, comments, "The Haroldsons are the greatest motivators to encourage you to pursue a postsecondary education and to inspire youth to become exemplary citizens of this country. Thanks to their participation many students are attending some of the best universities in the United States and receiving some of the best scholarships in the nation. For example, in the last six years, five of our students have received the Bill and Melinda Gates Scholarship."[194]

For several years John and María have been working with the U.S. Hispanic Leadership Institute, which is centered in Chicago and is the largest Latino student leadership organization in the country. Their initial challenge was to organize the first Oregon delegation to a national conference, which took place in Chicago, Illinois, in 2010. Two years later, they helped bring a regional conference for seven states to Portland, Oregon, and then they organized a delegation for the next national conference. Rocío de los Santos is serving as a volunteer for that delegation, and her younger sister will be a participant. She admits to having some doubts before she met the Haroldsons: "The first time I was informed about the Haroldsons' attendance at one of the meetings, I imagined them being the 'stuck-up Latinos' who show up just because it's their job. As soon as I walked into that room I got this comfortable sensation as if I had known them my entire life."[195] Rocío was even more impressed when María went to Rocío's house to discuss a problem that had come up with a group of students, and then kept in touch in order to check up on their progress. According to Rocío, "This act of showing up at our house gave the students an extra push to not give up on their goals, and they were comforted to know that

194 E-mail sent to me by Mario A. Magaña on 29 Dec 2012.
195 E-mail sent to me by Rocío de los Santos on 30 Dec 2012.

they are not going to be alone through this journey."[196]

John and María have presented internationally as well, participating in the Conference of Western Attorneys General Alliance Partnership, which helps train Mexican judges and lawyers for the transformation of the Mexican judicial system from written to oral advocacy.[197] John explains procedures followed in the U.S. judicial system to ensure fairness, and María focuses on victims' rights and how to prepare victims for testifying in court. "As children of immigrants," explains John, "it has given us a chance to go back full circle and be presenters in our heritage language, which as a couple has really been a powerful experience." María observes, "It's an opportunity to touch, smell and taste our roots... It reminds me of who I am and where I come from."

## Trials and tribulations of a District Attorney

Although his position is elected, John does not define himself as a campaigner. "I've always considered myself more of a prosecutor than a politician," he affirms. "My approach has been to be true to myself and what I believe in and the community will respond to that in a positive way."[198] During the ceremony when John was sworn in for his second elected term as district attorney, he gave a speech acknowledging his understaffed deputy D.A. team, local law officers and politicians, and especially his wife: "My wife has inspired every aspect of my life, and I can't imagine being where I am, and having done what I've done, without her." [199]

As a prosecutor, John has shown sensitivity to victims and their families and has consulted with them before agreeing to plea

---

196 Ibid.
197 Gillespie 1/1.
198 Neznanski 1/1.
199 Haroldson 2 Jan 2013.

bargains. One of his high-profile cases involved the prosecution of Joel Courtney for the 2004 rape and murder of Brooke Wilberger. The perpetrator directed authorities to her remains in order to avoid a possible death sentence. Brooke's parents agreed to the arrangement, and John praised them in a news report: "[The Wilbergers] modeled what is best in all of us. They have been consistently strong in the face of tragedy." [200] This case garnered national publicity and put John in the public eye. There was intense scrutiny of the way he handled the case, but John was undaunted: "There was significance beyond my accomplishment, as the first Latino D.A., for all of those who come after me. Big cases like that give me a strong sense of collectivism, which is the fiber of our cultural fabric."

Just as Sonia Sotomayor was criticized when she was an assistant D.A., John has received his share of potshots for putting people behind bars. He echoes Sonia's comment that a disproportionate number of crime victims are minorities, and their only hope of obtaining any compensation is through the legal system. "People who do not know me," he explains, "think that I am creating obstacles to positive social change. I try to demonstrate who I am through my work, so they can better understand me as a person and realize that I am fighting for justice for everybody."[201]

During a sentencing hearing for a 2012 double-murder case, John showed respect for the victims' family by not showing grisly photographs of the crime; instead, he displayed pictures of the victims when they were alive.[202] This case was particularly difficult for the prosecutor, since the confessed killer is from Peru and John would prefer to see Hispanics in the headlines for positive reasons. John also was involved in two local drug trafficking cases, dubbed

200 Schabner 2/2.
201 Statement made in a private conversation with me on 7 May 2013.
202 Fuqua 2/2.

"Icebreaker I and II," in which the majority of the defendants were Latinos. When he has to prosecute such cases, John states:

> It's very personal to me because I think of all the people who suffer as a result of the fuel that such individuals provide for negative stereotypes. I think individuals who engage in this type of criminal conduct do not define us as a community.... I have spoken publicly to say "this is not who we are. It represents an individual who chose to engage in criminal activity."... The reality is that there isn't a disproportionate number of Latinos who are the perpetrators of these crimes; that's not the case.

When María first began to work with John, she observed his work ethic, his discipline, and his dedication to social justice. According to her:

> John was one of the few prosecutors who always took time out to talk to the victim, and really listen to the victim. As a victim's advocate, I was impressed to see a prosecutor take time to validate the victim's experience, and to say as a male in a position of power, "what happened to you is an injustice, and there is a system by which you can experience justice, to a certain degree."

Besides being a strong advocate for the abolition of human trafficking, John is committed to ensuring equal opportunity access to justice for underrepresented minorities. As district attorney he has monitored the disproportional number of Latino crime victims and the underreporting of crimes against Latinos.[203] "The most difficult part of being a D.A.," he says, "is when you know that a crime occurred, but you don't have the evidence to prove it. That has a profound impact on the victim, and in many cases we are the only champions of the victim, so when we face that set of

---

203 OCHA website, accessed 29 Dec 12.

circumstances, it weighs heavily on my heart."

On the other hand, he also is very committed to ensuring that the accused are treated fairly: "One has to look at the big picture and have an understanding of cultural dynamics... For example, when you have an individual who is charged with possession of drugs but is also a victim of human trafficking, if we don't broaden our vision we might end up missing the target as far as justice is concerned." One of John's goals is to ensure that nobody is treated with favoritism, that no one receives a shorter or longer sentence because of their ethnic background. Another concern of his is that court interpreters be provided, and that they be competent. He remembers an arraignment in which an interpreter asked the accused if he pled guilty or not guilty, and the accused replied in Spanish, "Guilty?" The interpreter turned to the judge and declared, "He says guilty, Your Honor." Even though John was the prosecutor, he insisted: "As a bilingual officer of the court it is my duty to advise the court that the defendant's response was one of ambivalence. On behalf of the state, I would request that an attorney be appointed and a competent interpreter assigned so that the defendant can give a more meaningful response." John worries about what would have happened if he hadn't been there, and he is concerned that such miscarriages of justice are occurring throughout the country and to speakers of many different languages.

The cases that have the most personal resonance for John are the ones that involve child abuse, domestic violence, or hate crimes. He drafted a legislative proposal for the comprehensive reform of Oregon's hate crime policy. Two state representatives have transformed the proposal into a bill, and are co-sponsoring it.

In recognition of his dedication, John was honored by the Oregon Hispanic Bar Association with the 2011 Paul J. De Muniz Professionalism Award, named for the chief justice of the state

Supreme Court. According to the selection committee, John "exemplifies the spirit of professionalism, and has made significant contributions to the Latino community." [204]

Even though being a prosecutor is a very serious profession, John does have a lighter side. Besides having taught a salsa dance class and having performed in a community play, John loves to play the drums. He plays a blend of music, mostly rock 'n' roll from the 60s, but with elements of Mexican music, too. Moreover, he is familiar with 85 different knots for neckties, such as the half-Windsor and the Prince Albert. He can identify how somebody has tied his tie by looking at the knot. He doesn't use all 85 types of knots himself, however. "It's an art form," he says. "I pick my favorites and I go with that." John adores dogs, and he keeps two Labrador Retrievers in the office. The dogs are being trained by one of the staff members: one will be a trauma dog for crime victims and the other will be a service animal. In addition, the Haroldsons have two Chihuahuas that they keep at home, and they allow their pets to sleep in the bed with them.

## Latina activist and advocate

Before coming to Oregon, María Teresa had a vision that came to her repeatedly over a period of three years. She saw an image of an abandoned Latina child with abundant hair, covered with a white blanket that had pink flowers on it. Often, while riding in a car María would watch the side of the road, looking for that baby. When she was living in New Mexico, one day she went to pick up her daughter from school, saw something across the street and thought, "There she is." María ran over and picked up the baby, a Latina with thick hair, covered with a white blanket with pink flowers on it. The paramedics arrived and took the baby away, but

---

204 Ibid.

María was able to follow the case because of her job as a court-appointed advocate for children. She was pleased when the baby was adopted by a wonderful family. María Teresa believes that this incident was symbolic of her own imminent rebirth: her moving back to Oregon, getting her life back together, going back to school, and then beginning a more meaningful relationship with John Haroldson.

As part of her work with Crime Victims Units, María often helped women who could not speak English, were undocumented, and were victims of domestic abuse, sexual assault, or human trafficking. She worked to empower these women by helping them learn to navigate the judicial system and to break the cycle of abuse and victimization. As the owner of Culturally Responsive Solutions, María promotes an inclusive approach of inquiry and action to encourage the development of culturally sensitive and effective programs, policies and practices in the Corvallis school system and business community. She has done cross-cultural training for various organizations on the local and state levels, helping to ensure that the staff and policies are inclusive and that services are provided in an equitable manner. In her work with CASA (Court Appointed Special Advocates)-Voices for Children, María provided understanding and sympathy to abused and neglected children and tried to give them a voice in decisions regarding their wellbeing. She provided testimony in federal court and advocated for the rights of Latino children, who often are in foster care longer than others because of racial and cultural prejudices. She organized a popular event called "Midnight in Morocco" to recognize community members who have supported the cause of children in foster care. Due in part to her leadership, CASA was voted Nonprofit of the Year-2012.

In her current position at the Center for Latin@ Studies and Engagement at OSU (CL@SE), María works to promote and

135

encourage Latino students in regard to their education, future careers, and community involvement. One of her duties is to coordinate the ADELANTE program, which guides Latino students through a transformational leadership program. Susana Rivera-Mills, director of CL@SE and associate dean of the College of Liberal Arts at OSU, describes María and her work:

> María is an exceptional woman, who has a beautiful way of weaving her culture, gender, and life experience into everything she does. Her commitment to communities reflects her own realities as a Latina woman. She embodies CL@SE's mission and core values by providing a voice to populations that do not always have a voice in an academic setting, advocating for mutually beneficial partnerships between institutions and communities, and promoting culturally responsive approaches that recognize the value of popular knowledge and education into all formal environments.[205]

Over the past ten years, María has been on the board of directors or governing committee for a wide variety of organizations, including the OSU Board of Visitors on Minority Affairs, Oregon Crime Victim's Law Center, Oregon Attorney General's Sexual Assault Task Force, and Oregon Diversity Institute. She has served as a volunteer interpreter at a child abuse center, provided guidance to Latinos in the judicial system and with social services, served dinner to homeless people, organized events for Benton County nonprofits, and mentored high school, college, and university students. Recently she has helped a group of Latina high school students establish a club to provide mentorship and tutoring to elementary students.

María often has to juggle her personal and professional roles. She sometimes brings her grandchildren to social and political

---

205 E-mail sent to me by Susana Rivera-Mills on 2 Jan 2013.

events in order to provide them with an experiential learning opportunity. She attended one of her husband's swearing-in ceremonies on the same day as taking final exams. On another day, she took an exam and then helped her daughter give birth to her third child at home. "I was blessed with catching my grandson as he came out of the birth canal, and I received an A on the final exam that I took that day," María declares. With a smile, she adds: "I often combine international work assignments with intriguing and romantic getaways at wonderful hotels and restaurants as well as archeological visits."

## Defining activism and heroism

María believes that being an activist is "a lifestyle, a life choice, if you're someone who steps in when there's a need and you're selfless about it... I think a true activist is not egocentric, but group-centric. It's about groups, it's about community." John mentions the *Niños Héroes*, a group of teenage cadets who died defending Mexico during the Mexican-American War. "I thought that they were a classic example of the selfless collectivist value that permeated so much of what we grew up with and what we came to see as true heroism. The people I most admire are those who have dedicated their lives to reducing the strife and suffering in other people's lives." John offers Martin Luther King, César Chávez, and Ghandi as examples, and later mentions Dr. Juan Andrade, the president of the U.S. Hispanic Leadership Institute, whom he saw speak at OSU. Dr. Andrade's inspirational words reached the ears of a Latina student who had rejected her culture in order to blend into a small-town, predominantly white community. Afterwards, this young Latina exclaimed that she was going to sign up for the Hispanic Leadership Institute. "And how do you measure the impact of that?" asks John. "To say you have value, your culture has value, [there's] beauty in it. I know it sounds obvious, but the reality is that the internalized oppression that lingers is powerful and we don't speak of it. [Dr. Andrade] is a true hero, but he's a humble man."

John mentions his parents as sources of inspiration, as well as his maternal grandmother, who cared for wounded soldiers during the Mexican revolution. John describes her as "an incredibly tough, tough woman, and at the same time deeply philosophical." María believes that her mother is heroic. Her mother was an immigrant who taught herself English and learned how to interact effectively in western culture. Even though she was struggling to keep her family together, she would drop everything to help somebody else: a child who needed an advocate, a mother who needed assistance, or a homeless person. Her heroism also could be dramatic. "When a house was burning down in our neighborhood," exclaims María, "our mother didn't question it; she was a mother of ten children, but she ran in and brought two kids out. It wasn't a decision at that moment, it was the way she lived her life... it was beyond self."

### Challenges and ambitions

After completing her doctoral program, María plans to continue working for the benefit of Latino communities. John sees the need to create relationships of trust with minority communities in the area. One way the Haroldsons are doing that already is through their work with elementary through high school students, who may be inspired to pursue careers in public safety. "It's part of inspiring diversity through honest and meaningful interaction with communities that deserve our attention," he explains. "It's a continuous project. One of the challenges to attracting diverse candidates for job positions in Benton County is that the area is relatively homogenous, and that puts minority candidates in the role of pioneers, which can be stressful for families."

Although other positions have been suggested to John, such as being a judge, he prefers to focus on what he can do in his current role to make this a better world, and for him that means being an advocate for justice. Being a judge, according to John, is more like being an umpire, so a judge needs to strive for objectivity. One opportunity that he would like to have, however, is to contribute to taking constructive steps with Mexico to help build healthy relations with the United States so the two countries can improve together. "But frankly, " he declares, "whatever I do, my wife has to be part of it, because as much as I am willing to give, I cannot imagine accepting a position that would have us living apart from each other."

## Paying it forward

Both John and María acknowledge their debt to their families, their ancestors, and to the Latino community, and they are grateful for the opportunities that they have enjoyed. John observes: "We have seen generation after generation which has somehow given it all for the next generation. They've given it all, and maybe they could have kept a little more for themselves, but it was paid forward, everything was paid forward." Through their presentations and leadership programs, they hope to encourage the next generation to continue the process. This won't be easy, since activism has a degree of risk, according to María. "You can stay within your comfort zone, whatever that is, and you can be not speaking up, not standing in front of a crowd, not questioning authority, or you can take a risk, [and subject yourself to] the possibility for criticism, especially since you could be advocating for the undocumented population." For example, John and María were both very active in the campaign to get Oregon Senate Bill 833 passed and signed by the governor. They attended demonstrations, sat in on hearings, and lobbied legislators in order to influence the outcome. Governor

John Kitzhaber signed the bill into law on May 1, 2013, formally granting undocumented workers the right to obtain an Oregon driver's license.

María says that the love of her family keeps her going, and Latino pride is an important factor, too: "What helped me succeed through difficult times was calling upon my strong heritage and honing in on the fact that Latinos are survivors, adaptable under very difficult conditions, and we have centuries of history doing so." She feels that she is carrying her forefathers on her shoulders, and the inheritance they have given her is "the will to never give up, to keep moving forward no matter what, one foot in front of the other." John, having acknowledged his family, turns to María with a proud smile. "I don't mean to be trite," he says, "because this comes from my heart: María Teresa is the best blessing that I have ever had in my life and she has given me a sense of home, wherever I am, so together we have the energy to do the things that would have made our grandparents very proud of us."

María Teresa recognizes that her husband has made a significant difference in her life. "Being in a mutually respectful relationship is empowering!" she exclaims. "You lead your own life by choosing wisely…. Your relationship has everything to do with your success. If you're in a good relationship, you will have wings to fly; if you are not, you will flutter to the ground," she concludes.

Separately, both John and María are strong advocates for social change, but together they are an impressive force, much greater and much more dynamic than the sum of their parts. The work that they are doing will continue to ripple outward as the leaders they train and the students they encourage to become lawyers continue to step up and take their place in society.

§ § §

## Sources

(All websites accessed Jan-Feb 2013.)

de los Santos, Rocío. E-mail sent 30 Dec 2012.

Fuqua, Canda. "Man Sentenced to 2 Life Terms." Corvallis Gazette-Times, 10 Dec 2012. http://www.gazettetimes.com.

García, Kay S. "Interviews with John Haroldson and María Chávez-Haroldson." Recorded 5 Nov 2012 and 4 Jan 2013. Unpublished.

Gillespie, Emily. "Working for Justice." Corvallis Gazette-Times, 15 Mar 2011. http://www.gazettetimes.com.

Haroldson, John. Speech for swearing in ceremony for Benton County District Attorney and Deputy Attorneys, Benton County Courthouse, 2 Jan 2013.

Magaña, Mario A. E-mail sent 29 Dec 2012.

Neznanski, Matt. "Benton D.A. Eyes Federal Post." Albany Democrat-Herald, 29 Sep 2009. http://www.democratherald.com.

Oregon Commission on Hispanic Affairs, 2011 Annual Report. http://www.oregon.gov.

Oregon Voter's Guide, 2012. http://www.oregonvotes.org.

Rivera-Mills, Susana. E-mail sent 2 Jan 2013.

Schabner, Dean, and Sarah Netter. "Brooke Wilberger Found: Killer Gives Location of Remains to Avoid Death Penalty." ABC News website, 21 Sep 2009. http://abcnews.go.com.

# Sandra Cisneros

Kay (Kayla) S. García

## Chapter Five

## Sandra Cisneros: Literary Ambassador and Social Activist

"I mean to raise hell, and I think my stories do."

--Sandra Cisneros

"I believe that great writers are put on the planet to serve their community."

--Sandra Cisneros

Sandra Cisneros is a feisty and entertaining author whose physical appearance –long, flowing black hair, expressive eyes and sassy red lips, large hoop earrings, Buddhalupe tattoo (Virgin of Guadalupe sitting in the Lotus position) on her arm, embroidered blouse, jeans, cowboy boots— reflects some of the complexity, beauty and cultural authenticity of her writing.  She stands out as one of the most recognized Latina authors in the dynamic generation of writers identified with the term "Xicanisma."[206]  In the 1970s, male writers in the Chicano Movement such as Tomás Rivera, Rudolfo Anaya, and Rolando Hinojosa began to see their works published, but women in the movement were struggling to find a voice, according to numerous Latina scholars.  A decade later, Chicana authors started writing stories that questioned the dominance of men in the Latino culture and created new role

206 For more information on Xicanisma, see Ana Castillo's *Massacre of the Dreamers: Essays on Xicanisma.*

143

models for young women. Throughout the decade of the 80s, works by Ana Castillo, Gloria Anzaldúa, Denise Chávez, Cherríe Moraga and several others were being published by small Latino presses, when suddenly Sandra Cisneros broke into the mainstream consciousness with the publication by Random House of *Woman Hollering Creek and Other Stories* (1991). In 1994, a new edition of her already-popular novel, *The House on Mango Street,* and a six-figure advance for her collection of poems, *Loose Woman,* were enough to cement Sandra's[207] reputation as a successful writer who appeals to a large audience. Although she writes from the perspective of a Latina who grew up in a poor Chicago neighborhood, she speaks to people of all backgrounds. Her frank portrayal of the daily struggles and dangers of the *barrio* (Latino neighborhood), as well as the strength and resilience of some of its inhabitants, provides a stark contrast to both negative stereotypes and idealized representations like the neighborhood on *Sesame Street.* Although most of her work is set in Chicago, San Antonio, or Mexico City, against these backdrops she addresses universal themes such as love, death, and living life intensely. Sandra's literary works reflect her deep commitment to her community, to telling the personal stories that otherwise might not be told, and to conveying powerful sociopolitical messages. "I want people to really think about what I am saying," she insists, "to move them in a very visceral way."[208] Moreover, she frequently steps away from her computer in order to participate in real-life advocacy and community building.

Sandra's activism has included giving free workshops and literary readings to support her causes, organizing peace vigils, and speaking to students and community members at libraries,

---

207 I ask Sandra's and the reader's forgiveness for the use of her first name. I have done so in an attempt to get close to my subject, and to help the reader identify with her.
208 Shea 3.

schools and universities. She is the creator of two foundations that support socially-engaged writers, and she sponsors several literary awards and a writer-in-residency program. In order to help Our Lady of the Lake University in San Antonio recover from a devastating fire, she served as a volunteer writer-in-residence at that institution for several years. Sandra's causes include promoting Latino and other minority communities, women's rights, gay rights, and progressive political organizations. More recently she has taken a stand against capital punishment, particularly because it is used disproportionately against minorities. Furthermore, she has expanded her vision to include the global community, and she is interested in helping people understand the connections that exist among citizens in all the countries of the world.

Sandra's writing includes poetry (*Bad Boys, My Wicked Wicked Ways, Loose Woman*), a bilingual children's book (*Hairs/Pelitos*), two novels *(The House on Mango Street, Caramelo)*, a picture book for adults, *(Have You Seen Marie?)*, and several essays. Her first novel, *The House on Mango Street*, has sold over two million copies and is included in the curriculum of schools and universities throughout the United States. Although she has not escaped the sting of occasional criticism, her work has enjoyed both critical and popular success in the United States and abroad and has been translated into twelve languages. She has received several prestigious literary grants as well as an honorary doctorate, and her books have been awarded a long list of significant prizes. Two of her works have been adapted as plays -one performed in Chicago and the other in Dallas- and Lourdes Portillo has worked with Sandra on a screenplay for *The House on Mango Street.*

All of Sandra's work deals in some way with the challenges and complexities of growing up on the border between two cultures. She has "upended the mainstream literary canon," according to Diana Badur, "and has offered a sometimes painful recollection of what it takes to balance two cultures and the clash that results when they come into contact with each other."[209] Sandra's stories are based on her own experiences as well as those of her friends, family, and community. Carmen Rivera affirms that "[By] inserting her language, culture, histories, and worldviews into the American literary scene, Sandra Cisneros provides an accurate, comprehensive, and richer portrayal of the creativity and experience of Latina women and a heightened awareness of an inclusive, multicultural American literary tradition."[210]

### The sister of six swans

Sandra's father, Alfredo Cisneros del Moral, grew up in Mexico City in a family that had once been wealthy and continued to cling to aristocratic traditions.[211] Alfredo squandered his first year at the Mexican national university and fled to the United States in order to escape his father's wrath. He did not have proper documentation, so when he was apprehended he chose to join the U.S. army rather than risk deportation. Alfredo served during World War II, and when he returned to this country he visited Chicago, where he met Sandra's mother, Elvira Cordero Anguiano, at a dance. Elvira had grown up on the Near West Side of Chicago in a family of Mexican immigrants. Her father had come to the United States during the Mexican revolution (1910-1920) to work on the railroads. Eventually he was able to bring his family to Chicago, where he continued to work for the train system. Elvira

---

209 Badur 137.

210 Rivera 101.

211 Since most of this biographical information is widely available on websites and in various articles and books (listed in the Bibliography), I only have footnoted the quotes, and the passages that offer a unique perspective.

was never encouraged to study, so she dropped out of high school and began working at a factory, where she continued working for some years after getting married.

Sandra was born in Chicago on December 20, 1954, and was raised in a series of bleak, rundown *barrios* usually in third-floor apartments with communal stairs reeking of pine sol, and mice skittering around at night.  She had two older brothers and four younger ones; her only sister died when Sandra was very young, leaving her as the "odd girl out," since her brothers paired off and didn't want to be seen with her outside of the house.  Sandra has lamented her fate as the only daughter, and as *only* a daughter, since she believed that her father would have preferred to have seven sons.  She was treated as a little princess, so pampered and controlled by her father and brothers that she felt as though she had seven fathers.[212]   Sandra dreamed of being the sister in the "Six Swans" fairy tale, in which a young girl had to rescue her six brothers who had been turned into swans by an evil spell.  "Was it no coincidence my family name translated 'keeper of swans'?  I [also] dreamed myself Andersen's 'Ugly Duckling.' Ridiculous, ugly, perennially the new kid.   But one day the spell would wear off," she wrote.[213]   The spell did wear off, and now she travels around the country, using her story of being an awkward, lonely girl who struggled in school as a reminder to young people that they are not forever stuck where they are.  They can use the present time to change the future, altering their own fate as well as that of their community.

Sandra's isolation was exacerbated by her father's desire to return to Mexico almost every summer.  They would put furniture in storage, pack everything else in their car, and drive to Mexico City to stay at her grandparents' house.  There they were all ruled by her domineering grandmother, whose fictional counterpart

212 Bruns 123-124.
213 "Ghosts and Voices, Writing from Obsession" 71.

in *Caramelo* was given the moniker "the Awful Grandmother" because of her constant criticism of everybody.    Sandra has described her childhood as a series of "traumatic upheavals."[214] In Mexico she would be confronted with "not being truly Mexican," and at the end of the summer they would return to a different apartment, a new school, no friends, and the pain of "not being truly American."    She attended a public school for a year and a half, and from then on went to Catholic schools, where the nuns were "majestic at making one feel little"[215] and did not have high expectations for her.   In 1966 her parents borrowed enough money for a down payment on an old, rundown house in Humboldt Park, a multi-ethnic neighborhood on Chicago's North Side that included mainly Puerto Ricans, as well as Mexicans, Ukrainians, Poles, and other minorities.    This home, disappointing to her at the time, would become the setting for the fictional house on Mango Street. Poverty, loneliness, disillusionment, and the stresses of cultural hybridity are a few of the phantoms that motivate and inform Sandra's writing:    "I write about these ghosts inside that haunt me, that will not let me sleep, of that which even memory does not like to mention."[216]

Sandra sought refuge in the transformational power of fiction. Her mother took her to the local library every week in order to feed her voracious reading habit.  Sandra created a narrator in her head to glamorize the tedious details of her daily life, using her imagination to transform her environment: *"Thus clutching the coins in her pocket, our hero was off under a sky so blue and a wind so sweet she wondered it didn't make her dizzy."*[217]    She made drawings and wrote poems in a spiral notebook, which she took great pains to keep hidden.  Her mother, frustrated by her own lot

---

214 Ibid. 69.
215 Sagel 2/4.
216 "Ghosts and Voices, Writing from Obsession" 73.
217 Ibid. 70.

and wanting more for her daughter, encouraged Sandra to study and excused her from chores when she was doing homework. "I'm here because my mother let me stay in my room reading and studying, perhaps because she didn't want me to inherit her sadness and her rolling pin," she told a university audience.[218] Her father, too, encouraged her to pursue her education, but mainly as a means to finding a better husband. It was at Josephium High School, an all-girls Catholic institution, where a teacher gave Sandra her first recognition as a writer. Sandra began by reading her poetry in class, then became editor of the school's literary magazine, and had a few of her poems published in that journal. Her high school Spanish teacher introduced her to some of the great Spanish and Latin American poets: Federico García Lorca, Juan Ramón Jiménez, Pablo Neruda, Octavio Paz. She found a boyfriend for the first time, but that relationship was doomed because he wanted a traditional marriage and a house in the suburbs, plus he didn't understand why she wanted to be a writer.

## University years: rowing with a spoon and finding her oars

"I feel like I have been rowing a rowboat with a spoon," Sandra said, to describe her existence before some important truths came into focus for her and her life became less grueling.[219] She entered Loyola University in 1972 on scholarship, but had to take two subway trains and a bus each way for her daily commute from her family's home. She was the only Latina student majoring in English, and most of the required reading was by white male authors, despite the increasing visibility of "minority authors" such as the black writers Toni Morrison and Alice Walker, as well as some of the Chicano writers already mentioned (Rivera, Anaya, Hinojosa). Sandra turned to Emily Dickinson for inspiration and

---

218 "Notes to a Younger Writer" 75.
219 Kevane 54.

hope, not realizing until years later that Dickinson wrote from a privileged position. Her later comment about Dickinson's maid contains an eerie echo of the relationship between Sandra and her mother: "Maybe Emily Dickinson's Irish housekeeper had to sacrifice her life so that Emily could live hers locked upstairs in the corner bedroom writing her 1,775 poems."[220] When Sandra took a creative writing course during her junior year, she wrote stories about homeless people and alcoholics who slept in the park, foreshadowing her preoccupation with the marginalized characters of the *barrio*.

Sandra graduated from Loyola University in 1976 and won a scholarship to attend the prestigious University of Iowa Writer's Workshop, where she began work on a Master's degree in creative writing. It was here that Sandra first understood, and confronted, the exclusivity of the mainstream literary canon, which to her seemed like the discourse of privilege. "I am a writer *despite* the Iowa Writer's Workshop," Sandra said in an interview. "It taught me what I didn't want to be as a writer, and how I didn't want to teach."[221] At first she felt burdened by her social and economic disadvantages: "My classmates were from the best schools in the country. They had been bred as fine hothouse flowers. I was a yellow weed among the city's cracks."[222] A breakthrough moment came during a class discussion of Gaston Bachelard's *The Poetics of Space* and the use of "house" as a metaphor for the self. Sandra realized that, unlike her classmates, she did not have a safe and comfortable house with spacious stairways and multiple rooms, so the metaphor did not work for her. In all of her years of study, she had never encountered a description of a house like hers. "I realized my education had been a lie —had

---

220 "Notes to a Younger Writer" 75.
221 "Sandra Cisneros: I Hate the Iowa Writers' Workshop"
222 Sagel 3/4.

made presumptions about what was 'normal,' what was American, what was valuable— I wanted to quit school right then and there, but I didn't," she wrote. "Instead, I got angry, and anger when it is used to act, when it is used nonviolently, has power." [223]

Defiantly, she began to write about crowded apartments, scurrying rats, and drunken men hurling rocks through windows. By doing so, she discovered her own unique voice, and began to develop some of the stories that would appear in *The House on Mango Street.* In terms of Sandra's metaphor of rowing with a spoon, this discovery was equivalent to finding her oars. "I can say that my political consciousness began the moment I recognized my otherness...," she explained. "Once I could name [my otherness], I ceased being ashamed and silent."[224]

### Changing the world through education and writing

While she was in Iowa, Sandra made friends with the Native American poet Joy Harjo and discovered the works of other authors of color such as Maxine Hong Kingston (Asian American), Gary Soto (Chicano), and Toni Morrison (African American), who were all writing from the perspective of people who were labeled "ethnic minorities." She met more Latino writers during vacations when she returned to Chicago and began doing some poetry readings with the *Movimiento Artístico Chicano* (Chicano Artistic Movement). After completing her Master's in Fine Arts, Sandra moved back to Chicago and began teaching at an alternative high school in a Chicano neighborhood. Later she accepted a job as a recruiter and counselor at her alma mater, Loyola University, where she worked with minority and disadvantaged students. The students at both these institutions had stories that were even more

223 Introduction to *The House on Mango Street* (1994 edition) xiv.
224 Ibid. xiii – xvi.

heartwrenching than Sandra's. She wanted to change their lives, and she began writing vignettes that offered alternative paths for them. Some of these tales became part of *The House on Mango Street*. To this day, Sandra continues to be an ardent advocate for inclusive curriculum in public schools. She believes that Latinos need to read about their history and know who they are so that those who are disadvantaged can take pride in their identity and dream beyond the *barrio*. In addition, she has advocated for Planned Parenthood and the prevention of teen pregnancy, which she sees as a problem of low self-esteem. She believes that if young women are encouraged to believe in themselves and to seek opportunities for advancement, then they won't depend on the approval of boyfriends for self-affirmation. She wants women to plan their own lives. "First they've got to take care of their dreams," she insists, "and then maybe have babies later in life."[225]

As a teacher, Sandra struggled with the dilemma of trying to teach poetry to students who were experiencing hunger, overwhelming family responsibilities, and daily threats to their existence. According to her, she made a lot of mistakes at first, but an important breakthrough occurred when she applied what she had learned about writing to what she was doing as a teacher:

> Just as I had to find my writing voice, I also had to find my teaching voice. They both came from my center, from my passions, from that perspective that was truly mine and made me different from any other teacher. To get there I had to take the same circular route as writing. I had to be intuitive, and I had to be willing... to take risks and make mistakes, willing to meander off the track to get on the track, to change plans midstream if need be.[226]

---

225 "Sandra Cisneros: Community Activism"
226 "Foreword" x.

Sandra used class assignments to help students reflect on their own lives, and thus see possible alternatives to the paths chosen for them. Carol Jago, in her book *Sandra Cisneros in the Classroom*, describes how Jago herself does something similar by using Sandra's work to inspire students to write about their own lives. The students recognize the truth in Sandra's writing, and are inspired to use writing to tell their own truths. The results can be impressive: "Sandra Cisneros' stories have changed the world," Jago declares. "An outrageous assertion? Maybe. But reflecting on the impact *The House on Mango Street* has had on students at my high school over the past decade, I have come to believe that one slim volume can indeed alter our angle of repose."[227] Besides the benefit of self-reflection, the students experience an important affirmation when someone else reads their words. While discussing her student Brian, who lived with the constant threat of gang violence, Jago explains, "I know that there is a kind of salvation in reading and writing.... It seemed to me that, while providing guidance for his poetry writing would be useful, what Brian needed most from me was simply to bear witness."[228]

While making progress with her students, Sandra continued to read her poetry in local coffeehouses, where she was noticed by someone from the Chicago Transit Authority's poetry project. Soon her words were being read by thousands of bus and subway riders. This caught the attention of the writer Gary Soto, who helped her get a brief collection of poems, *Bad Boys*, published by Mango Press. These poems reflected her early observations and feelings about life in the *barrio*, and most of them were reprinted in later collections or transformed into stories.

## The House on Campbell Street

Although her poetry was becoming known, Sandra did not

227 Jago xi.
228 Ibid. 37.

have much time to work on her fiction. In 1982 a grant from the National Endowment for the Arts allowed her to quit her job and focus on writing her stories, which she did first in Provincetown, Massachusetts, and later on a Greek island. She took some time to visit France, Yugoslavia, and other European countries, and then served for a while as artist-in-residence at the Michael Korolyi Foundation in Venice, Italy. She returned to the United States just before the release of her book by Arte Público Press, which she called *The House on Mango Street*. This title reflected the spirit of the book better than the actual name of the street in Humboldt Park where Sandra lived as a child, which was Campbell Street. Begun in 1977 and completed in 1982, this collection of poetic vignettes presents a strikingly honest and realistic portrait of the *barrio*. It is both a collection of stories and a coherent novel, since each story makes sense on its own and also contributes to the whole. The narrator is appropriately named Esperanza, which means "hope" in English. She helps the reader recognize the hope that is hidden under the gritty and dangerous surface of the *barrio*, where life is an endless struggle but people persist, and some manage to succeed in spite of the threefold impediments of racism, sexism and poverty. An important message of the book is that those who do make it out of there should return to the neighborhood to help others.

*The House on Mango Street* was praised by most reviewers and even won the Columbus Foundation's American Book Award in 1985. The writer Robin Ganz explained the book's appeal: "[As] with the clearest water, beneath the surface, Cisneros' work is alive with complexity and depth of meaning. Cisneros' voice is the sound of many voices speaking —over the kitchen table, out on the street, across the borderlands, and through the years."[229] Soon this novel became part of the curriculum in schools and universities throughout the nation, in Women Studies, Ethnic

229 Quoted in Bruns 131.

Studies, English, Creative Writing, Sociology, and even Sex Education. Some "defenders of the canon" objected, of course, but to no avail. Sandra's acceptance as a writer was an important step in the journey toward a more inclusive environment in which the literary and cultural value of writing by ethnic minorities is recognized.

Many critics have focused on this novel as an autobiographical coming-of-age story whose preteen protagonist, Esperanza, is sometimes wise beyond her years. The author is quick to point out that Esperanza is based not only on her own experiences, but also on those of her family, neighbors, and students, and thus provides a collective story of a Latino community. She wants her readers to recognize their responsibility to their own community, so in response to the frequent question of whether or not she is Esperanza, she has replied, "Am I Esperanza? Yes. And no.... One thing I know for certain, you, the reader, are Esperanza... What happened to you? Did you...learn to be the human being you are not ashamed of?... Did you get angry? *You* are Esperanza. You cannot forget who you are." [230] Thus, just as Esperanza is exhorted by another character to return to her community to help others, readers, too, are goaded in the direction of social activism. On a deeper level, this novel is about an author in her twenties who is developing sociopolitical awareness and is recognizing herself as "the other." While defining her own difference by describing the harsh realities of the barrio, she makes it possible for non-Latinos to appreciate their mutual humanity: "I want people to recognize themselves in 'the other' in my characters. I think that once you see yourself in the other, in that person who is most unlike you, then the story has done its political work. Then we cease to be

---

230 Introduction to *The House on Mango Street* (1994 edition) xix-xx.

a 'they' or 'that' or 'those kind,' and we become humans. That recognition restores people their humanity, which is the big goal."[231]

## An indestructible home in the heart

"The work is always wiser than the writer," Sandra said, "[because] there are things in the text that the characters said that came true."[232] In *The House on Mango Street*, a "witchwoman" tells Esperanza that she will have a "home in the heart." Years later, Sandra understood what she meant: "I realize who I am, [I] feel very, very strong and powerful, I am at peace with myself and I don't feel terrified by anyone, or by any terrible word that anyone would launch at me from either side of the border. I guess I've created a house of bricks that no big bad wolf can blow down now."[233]

Sandra started building that house of bricks when she left her family's home and started creating a new lifestyle for herself as an independent woman. She faced bitter criticism from her father and brothers, who regarded her as a traitor to her family and to her culture. She was scorned by some authors, such as the Latino writer who accused Sandra and others who attend "fancy workshops" of using their craft to disparage the Latino people.[234] She was denigrated for writing about her own brand of spirituality, which differed greatly from traditional Catholicism. "Unless I make somebody angry, I realize I'm not doing my job," she quipped. So many insults were hurled at Sandra that she started redefining those terms to fit her own perspective, just as the LGBTQ community has appropriated traditionally derogatory words like "queer." Thus she gave her first book-length volume

231 Shea 4.
232 Ibid.  4.
233 Aranda 74.
234 Mirriam-Goldberg 80.

156

of poetry the ironic and mocking title *My Wicked Wicked Ways*. Begun as a Master's thesis when Sandra was at the Iowa Writer's Workshop and published in 1987, this collection received positive reviews for the poetry. However, the cover of the book kicked off a controversy because of the photo of Sandra sitting cross-legged, wearing a low-cut dress, red earrings, red lipstick, and cowboy boots, with cigarette in hand and a glass of wine by her side. Some feminists, who criticized her for posing like cheap cheesecake, missed the *picardía* and irony of her dressing up that way while posing for the cover of her own book of poetry. *Picardía* is a very Mexican type of humor, based on double meanings and brazen sexuality. "Where's their sense of humor?" Sandra asked. She saw it as a "fun photo," meant as both homage and parody of old-time film stars like Rita Hayworth, who provided rare glimpses of feminine power when Sandra was a child.[235]

Both the title and the cover photo indicate that the poet is attempting to trespass the boundaries established by her family, society, and the Catholic church. Sandra has said that Latinas wrestle with a lot of guilt, calling herself the "worst censor of all." "I found it very hard to deal with redefining myself or controlling my own destiny or my own sexuality," Sandra explained, "...it's a ghost I'm still wrestling with."[236] According to her, you can't get rid of those ghosts, but you can make your peace with them. As the protagonist of *The House on Mango Street* explained, "I put it down on paper and then the ghost does not ache so much."[237] *My Wicked Wicked Ways* is Sandra's attempt to appropriate her sexuality and tell her story from her own point of view. In the preface written in free verse, she declares, "I took the crooked route and liked my badness." She then lists the wicked things she has done: "Played at mistress./ Tattooed an ass./ Lapped up

---

235 Ibid. 72; and Aranda 68.
236 Aranda 67.
237 *The House on Mango Street* 110.

my happiness from a glass/….[And] I left my father's house."[238]
The poems express the pain, disappointment, and sorrow of a
challenging childhood and young adulthood. They provide brief
portraits of friends, and describe the excruciating ecstasy of
an affair: "you my religion/and I a wicked nun."[239] There is an
occasional flicker of joy, such as in her poem about being alone
on an island: "To wander darkness like a man, Ilona./ My heart
stood up and sang."[240] (Ilona is a friend's name.) In another poem
she describes her confusing, oxymoronic persona: "I am an odd
geometry/ of elbows and skin,/ a lopsided symmetry of sin/ and
virtue."[241]

*My Wicked Wicked Ways* describes a Latina's search for
freedom; in her later volume, *Loose Woman* (1992), Sandra
finds that freedom. Sandra has called the former collection her
"wanderings in the desert," and has indicated that those poems
were influenced –and inhibited– by her formal training at the
Iowa Writers' Workshop. "There are tighter and tauter lines
in *My Wicked Wicked Ways*," she said. "It is more like ballet….
*Loose Woman* has a more colloquial flavor…. Everything is loose…..
It's like I got the workshop, the Church, and everybody else off
my back. It's a much looser, freer, jazzier voice in these newer
poems."[242] The title plays on the Spanish expression for poems that
have not been included in a collection, *poemas sueltos*, or loose
poems, but the wordplay only begins there. Sandra is reinventing
the insult "loose woman," and transforming it into a declaration
of independence: unattached, unencumbered, unfettered, set
free. The poems reflect the exhilaration and agony of intense
love, as well as the power that comes with knowing and loving
oneself. The poet Joy Harjo described this collection succinctly:

238 *My Wicked Wicked Ways* xi.
239 Ibid. 34.
240 Ibid. 44.
241 Ibid. 82.
242 Kevane 48.

"These poems are firecrackers and tequila, with a little candlelight and lace linen."[243] I would add this warning: Perhaps if you get up enough speed as you read these poems, you won't feel the flames burning you.

Sandra had moved to San Antonio in 1984 when she accepted a position as literary director for the Guadalupe Cultural Arts Center. Living in a town whose Mexican and Chicano traditions are reflected in a rich linguistic complexity -as well as in cuisine, festivals and architecture- had an energizing and liberating influence on Sandra's writing. *Loose Woman* begins with joyful images of asymmetry and imbalance, which were present in her earlier poems, but are more developed in this volume. The first poem reads, "Little clown, my heart,/ Spangled again and lopsided,/...Little gimp-footed hurray,/... Acapulco cliff-diver *corazón*,/...Alley-oop and here we go/Into the froth, my life,/Into the flames!"[244]

Sandra attacks stereotypes in "Mexicans in France," a dialogue with a French man: "Is it true/ all Mexicans/ carry knives?/ I laugh./ --Lucky for you/ I'm not carrying my knife/ today./ He laughs too./ --I think the knife you carry is abstract." In the more political poem "Sarajevo," Sandra expresses both her frustration and her solidarity with her friend Jasna, who was living in that city under siege: "At any moment/ a precise second might claim you./ ...I'm a woman like you./ I don't count either./ Not a thing I say./ Not a thing I do." Fortunately, Sandra was able to do something that might have had some influence, since she managed to get a letter from Jasna published in all the major newspapers in this country, along with an article in which Sandra advocated for U.S. intervention. To further publicize her message, Sandra organized weekly peace vigils until Sarajevo was liberated from the siege.

---

243 Quoted in Mirriam-Goldberg 93.
244 *Loose Woman*. I have identified poems from this volume by title rather than page number.

In a more gentle poem, "Arturito the Amazing Baby Olmec Who Is Mine by Way of Water," Sandra sings the praises of her godson and makes three wishes for him: that he be noble like the revolutionary leader Emiliano Zapata, wise like Gandhi, who "knew the power of the powerless," and generous like Mother Teresa, "Because the way of wealth is giving/ yourself away to others."

The final, eponymous poem of the collection establishes a striking "they say/I say" dichotomy: "They say I'm a *macha*, hell on wheels,/ *viva-la-vulva*, fire and brimstone,/ man-hating, devastating,/ boogey-woman lesbian./ Not necessarily, but I like the compliment." The poem climaxes with her powerful self-definition: "I'm an aim-well,/ shoot-sharp,/ sharp-tongued,/ sharp-thinking,/ fast-speaking,/ foot-loose,/ loose-tongued,/ let-loose,/ woman-on-the-loose/ loose woman./ Beware, honey."

During the same time she was writing the poems of *Loose Woman*, Sandra was working on *Woman Hollering Creek and Other Stories*. The brief biography at the end of this book describes her as "nobody's mother and nobody's wife," a phrase that has been used as further confirmation of her shameless independence. According to Roger Bruns, "this book expanded the horizon of voices and added new layers of society in the stories." Bruns points out that Sandra functions like a ventriloquist, capturing the tone and feeling of each character in their own voices.[245] Sandra was trying to represent the entire spectrum of the Latino community, and to do that she continued to experiment with unusual and fascinating combinations of the Spanish and English languages. The first part of the book focuses on children, revisiting some of the themes presented in *The House on Mango Street*. The second half of the book delves deeply into the adult world while still drawing from childhood memories in an attempt to create a fictional homeland. "I was also working on the sense of memory from my childhood that helped to create an invented Mexico, an

245 Bruns 134.

imaginary Mexico, an imaginary homeland as Salmon Rushdie would say," explained Sandra.[246]  Sandra could not go back to the actual Mexico of her childhood, since everything had changed. In the story "Tepeyac," referring to the neighborhood where the author's grandparents lived, the protagonist returns to the site of her *abuelito's* (grandfather's) store, which had been converted to a pharmacy, leaving nary a trace of the former business.  "[Abuelito, you] took with you to your stone bed something irretrievable, without a name."[247]

Several of the stories in *Woman Hollering Creek* convey a powerful message to women to stop being so passive and to stop trying to conform to society's expectations. The story "Little Miracles, Kept Promises" consists of a series of letters of supplication or gratitude to the Virgin of Guadalupe, the spiritual mother of Mexicans on both sides of the border.  In some Latin American communities, *machismo*, or the belief that men are superior to women, has a female counterpart called *marianismo*, which is the acceptance by women of their submissive role, in emulation of the Virgin Mary (or her Mexican manifestation, Guadalupe).  In Sandra's story, the Virgin is depicted as a Great Spirit that could be called Buddha or many other religious names, and she is a source of inspiration and strength rather than a perpetuator of women's subjugation. One of the characters in the story, a young girl who wants to be a painter, leaves a note to the Virgin explaining her rebellious attitude: "I wasn't going to be my mother or my grandma.  All that self-sacrifice, all that silent suffering.  Hell no.  Not here.  Not me."[248]

In the story, "*Bien* Pretty," the protagonist dreams of slapping the heroines of *telenovelas* (Latin American soap operas) to their senses so that they would wake up and stop being so passive:  "I

246 Kevane 51.
247 *Woman Hollering Creek* 23.
248 Ibid. 127.

want them to be women who make things happen....Real women. The ones I've loved all my life.... Passionate *and* powerful, tender and volatile, brave. And, above all, fierce."[249] The narrator wants women to "relive that living when the universe ran through the blood like river water. Alive.... I mean live our lives the way lives were meant to be lived. With the throat and wrists. With rage and desire, and joy and grief, and love till it hurts, maybe. But goddamn, girl. Live."[250]

The eponymous story "Woman Hollering Creek" is a transformation of the Mexican legend of *La Llorona*, a woman who drowned her children centuries ago and still gives people the chills with her haunting cries. In Sandra's version, the *Llorona* figure is a modern-day Mexican woman who manages to escape from her abusive husband. The pregnant protagonist (Cleófilas) and her son get a ride to the bus station from Felice, a happily single Latina who drives a red pickup truck. Cleófilas is impressed by Felice's strength and independence, but surprised that Felice is content alone, and not beholden to any man. Even though Cleófilas obviously has a long, difficult path ahead of her, she learns from Felice an important lesson about self-confidence and the celebration of life. Her own child and unborn baby are with her, not drowned in the creek and not left at the mercy of their violent father. The name of the creek in Spanish is *"La Gritona,"* or yelling woman. Sandra has been called *gritona*, and described as "a Latina writer screaming out loud to all who will listen."[251]

## A one-person peace demonstration

Sandra, who drives a red pickup and insists on remaining

---

249 Ibid. 161.
250 Ibid. 163.
251 Badur 138.

single, based the strong Latina character Felice on herself. In her second novel, *Caramelo* (2003), she creates a protagonist who also has a lot in common with her, a young Latina named Celaya who gradually develops her own voice and identity. Celaya, like Sandra, has six brothers and belongs to a commuter family that travels periodically between Chicago and Mexico, with a brief stay in San Antonio, Texas. Sandra has said that she intended this book to be a healing medicine for our society's climate of violence and fear. "I could be a one-person peace demonstration," she said. "I could work nonviolently for communities to come together and understand each other."[252] Thus, she hopes her novel will change her readers' attitudes and actions. "It creeps up on you like a Trojan horse. You take it home, you think about it, and you suddenly realize that you look at the world in a different way. It's much more persuasive than bonking someone over the head with a big peace sign."[253]

A *caramelo* is a kind of *rebozo* or shawl, and in the novel Sandra has woven together the stories of four generations, whose characters interact with the *caramelo* by wearing, storing, or gifting it, plaiting and unplaiting the fringe as a form of silent communication, or sucking on the fringe for comfort. *Caramelo* is also a kind of burnt sugar candy, like caramel, whose rich sweetness could symbolize all the ways in which Mexico overstimulates the senses and enhances one's sensation of being alive. "The memories that Cisneros offers in this book sometimes wrinkle the nose and scorch the palate," according to one reviewer.[254] Caramel is the skin color of the washerwoman's daughter Candelaria, who turns out to be Celaya's half-sister, a sibling she missed knowing -like the deceased sister of the author herself- a symbol of the

---

252 Vidimos 1-2/3.
253 Ibid. 2/3.
254 *San Francisco Chronicle*, 15 Dec 2002, quoted on Sandra Cisneros's website.

greater Mexican family that Celaya couldn't embrace because of social, linguistic and geographic barriers. *Caramelo* portrays the Mexico that doesn't exist, the country that Sandra had to invent, since she was caught hovering in space over the border between the U.S. and Mexico, unable to touch down and take ownership of either country.

The novel's characters trace the paths of great immigrations, from North Africa to Spain, Spain to Mexico, and Mexico to the United States. Celaya's great-grandfather from Seville has features that reveal his Berber heritage, her grandparents and father are Mexican, and her mother is Mexican-American. Family conflicts break out due to differences in gender, class, nationality, and generation. Mexican film stars, historical figures, dancers, and a ventriloquist show up and interact with the fictional characters. The historical references and popular icons are explained in copious footnotes, which also reveal more of the family history, while adding to the hopscotch nature of the discourse. The novel acquires additional complexity when the "Awful Grandmother" protests the way in which Celaya is telling her story. The grandmother's spirit manages to take over the narrative to tell her own side of the story, and thus generates some compassion for this cantankerous character.

Although the novel does present the harsh realities of daily life on both sides of the border, the main messages of the book are an affirmation of the value of each culture, the courage of immigrants in a foreign land, and the sanctity of the Latino family. Sandra wrote this book to honor her father, and to celebrate the remarkable spirit of immigrants in the United States. Although her mother's story is not featured in the book, her voice is present, according to Sandra: "My mother's voice is the one of immigrant children who have had to fight for themselves in the streets of Chicago. She has helped me to create Latina characters who are very anti-stereotypical."[255]

*Caramelo* opens with a description of a family photo that did not include Celaya. Her family was on a beach in Acapulco and did not notice she was missing. From this place of "not existing," Celaya slowly builds her sense of self by telling the family history and thus, ironically, she saves all of her family members from oblivion. As she narrates, she grows into a self-confident young woman, capable of recovering quickly from a failed romance, and observing, "Ernesto. He was my destiny, but not my destination."[256] Her strength and maturity are evident in a scene reminiscent of Gabriel García Márquez'ss works of magic realism[257]: as her *papá* lies in a hospital bed, Celaya barters with her grandmother's ghost for a little more time with her father.

In real life, Sandra's father was dying as she was writing *Caramelo*, and she commented in an interview that she wished she could negotiate for more time with him, as her fictional counterpart did. Sandra's father died in 1996, and a year later, still depressed by her loss, she decided to brighten her life by painting her house purple, with turquoise trim. This created quite a stir in her historic neighborhood, and she garnered national attention by holding a press conference on her front lawn. She insisted that the bright colors were a historically correct reflection of Latino culture, and "after all," she said, "it's the city of San Antonio, and not Saint Anthony."[258] The controversy dragged on long enough for the paint to fade to blue, a color that was officially approved for that neighborhood.

---

255 Kevane 54.
256 *Caramelo* 399.
257 Magic realism is a literary style that combines detailed descriptions of daily life with supernatural characters or events.
258 Bruns 137.

### Bibliotherapy: *Have You Seen Marie?*

Sandra was very close to her father, and mourned intensely and for a long period of time after his death. However, in spite of her mother's sacrifices (or maybe because of them), she did not get along very well with her. Thus, Sandra was surprised at the acute pain she felt years later when her mother passed away. One way that she dealt with that anguish was the writing and public presentations of *Have You Seen Marie?* (2012), a picture book for adults illustrated by Ester Hernández. While telling the story of a search for a lost cat, the book portrays a multicultural San Antonio neighborhood and the colorful characters who live there, and explores the possibility of maintaining spiritual and sensorial connections to a departed loved one.

Sandra believes that by using books for healing, a process she calls "bibliotherapy," she is carrying on a tradition of her indigenous ancestors who regarded stories as medicine. "I think all books are medicine, and they are meant for a person who has an ailment of a certain kind.... So my story was one about my mother's death, dealing with her absence, and transforming that grief into light," Sandra explained.[259] Her readers, too, could use the book to help deal with loss, as could the spectators at her public presentations. When she reads her work, she acts out parts of the story and modulates her voice to imitate each character's way of speaking. She uses a deep, gravelly voice for the River, who says he has seen *everything* because his water makes its way around the entire world, "washing away the dead... bringing new life, the salty and the sweet, mixing with everything, everything, everything, everything."[260] The River's words of wisdom allow the protagonist to see, hear and feel her mother's presence. In the Afterword,

---

259 Macias 1/2.
260 *Have You Seen Marie?* 73.

the author explains, "I wish somebody had told me love does not die, that we continue to receive and give love after death."[261] However, this consolation is not a simple solution: "There is no getting over death, only learning how to travel alongside it. It knows no linear time. Sometimes the pain is as fresh as if it just happened. Sometimes it's a space I tap with my tongue daily like a missing molar."[262] When the pain is overwhelming, Sandra observes that it's helpful to draw, paint, sing or do anything else that is creative: "It's essential to create when the spirit is dying. It doesn't matter what."[263]

### Giving back

Even though she has two college degrees, Sandra chose to be poor because she wanted to write. "Whenever a job took too much of my time, I would quit," she declared. "It's meant a lot of sacrifices."[264] Sandra limited her employment, restricted her relationships, and never had children. Her priorities were clear: "My writing is my child and I don't want anything to come between us," she said.[265] Sandra considered it her duty not only to bear witness to how people in her community lived, but also to inject her vision of how they could do better. By creating alternate endings to some of her character's life stories, she actually may have helped some readers reflect on their lives and take control of their own destinies. Her writing has provided hope and inspiration to countless students, thanks to teachers like Carol Jago, whose book *Sandra Cisneros in the Classroom* has facilitated the incorporation of Sandra's poems and stories into

---

261 Ibid. 91.
262 Ibid. 94.
263 Ibid. 93.
264 Aranda 70.
265 Ibid. 72.

the curriculum of schools and universities.

In support of Latinos and other minorities, Sandra has pressured businesses to be more inclusive in their hiring practices, urged publishers to be more open-minded when choosing which books to publish, and encouraged organizations to support a wider variety of artists. She has passed up lucrative speaking and commercial offers from organizations she considers discriminatory. To protect the innocent victims of war, she lobbied for U.S. intervention in Sarajevo by writing articles, making speeches, and holding peace vigils. Remembering the neighborhood library as her childhood refuge, Sandra has given talks and participated in fundraising efforts to help keep open the doors of local libraries. She has advocated for education reform, asserting that Latinos should have the opportunity to learn about their history and culture, and should be encouraged to maintain high expectations. Once they have achieved success, students should return to their communities to help others: "It's a circular thing," says Sandra, "you leave, but you also do other work to enable other people to control their destinies as well."[266] Sandra recommends that students try to remember their life in the *barrio*. "What you know at a very early age gives you empathy and compassion…. Use what you know to help heal the pain in your community."[267]

Sandra has supported the arts and struggling writers by giving free lectures and workshops, and organizing cultural events such as a book fair in San Antonio, which brought together many Latino authors, publishers and readers. She traveled to Chicago to help the YMCA dedicate the new Chernin Center for the Arts, which serves three low-income neighborhoods in Chicago. Sandra has made several efforts to organize groups that bring together people of different disciplines, generations, and sexual orientations. After receiving the prestigious MacArthur Award, she organized

266 Ibid. 70.
267 Benson F7.

some Latino recipients of that award into a coalition, called Los MacArturos, for the purpose of sharing their expertise with the community through workshops, readings, and performances. Sandra is the president and founder of the Macondo Foundation, an association of community-oriented writers who are committed to promoting nonviolent social change.[268] Macondo was initiated in 1995 and is named for the mythical setting of Gabriel García Márquez's definitive novel, *One Hundred Years of Solitude*. The Macondo Foundation sponsors literary workshops, a writer-in-residency program, and various grants, including one named for Sandra's mother, the Elvira Cordero Cisneros Award. Sandra founded another organization to honor the memory of her father, the Alfredo Cisneros Del Moral Foundation, which awards grants to authors who write about or have lived in Texas. In addition, Sandra participated in a film project called "The Desert Is No Lady," to document and promote the work of Southwestern women artists.

Sandra has spoken of the despair she feels when she reads the news and realizes how much more needs to be done in our schools and in our society in general. "Yet now and again...," she concedes, "a single compassionate being confirms my belief in the generosity of the human spirit. It is a great and marvelous thing to be reminded that to change the world we need only to change ourselves."[269]

## Roadmaps for writers and activists

When she was in the sixth grade, Sandra started recording her thoughts and poems in a spiral notebook that she had to

268 Information on Sandra's foundations, the grants that she provides to other writers, and the fellowships and prizes she has received, can be found on her website.
269 "Foreword" xi-xii.

hide from her brothers. She developed into a precedent-setting author, receiving six-figure advances for her books in addition to substantial grants, such as the $250,000 MacArthur Foundation fellowship, known as the "genius grant." As the first Chicana author to publish a book with a mainstream publisher, she opened doors for other Latina writers and opened the minds of countless readers previously unfamiliar with life in the *barrio*. Writing at first from a place of anger and exclusion, she gradually developed into a literary ambassador between the Latino and Anglo worlds, defining herself as both an amphibian and a translator of cultures. She has told her stories from a woman's point of view, and brought female characters out of the shadows. She has described her work as that of a cartographer trying to fill in the gaps on the literary map: "I'm trying to write the stories that haven't been written. I feel like a cartographer; I'm determined to fill a literary void."[270]

Sandra has created liberating alternatives to some oppressive Latina archetypes, such as the Virgin of Guadalupe, La Malinche, and La Llorona. Her innovative use of language has enlivened her work. According to Sandra, there are two voices that surface in her writing: "my mother's punch-you-in-the-face English and my father's powdered-sugar Spanish."[271] She incorporates street slang and Spanglish into her writing, rebelling against formality: "It's in this rebellious realm of antipoetics that I tried to create a poetic text with the most unofficial language I could find. I did it neither ingenuously nor naturally. It was as clear to me as if I were tossing a Molotov." The rhythm of her writing sometimes reflects Spanish syntax, and she often translates Spanish idioms literally, creating new expressions in English. She includes some Spanish words that are repeated in English or explained by the context, while others are left to taunt —or haunt— the monolingual reader

---

270 Kevane 1/4.
271 "Ghosts and Voices, Writing from Obsession" 72.

(What does *abuelito* mean?).    She encourages young writers to listen to the voices around them, and to experiment with language in creative ways.

Sandra urges aspiring authors to become familiar with all of the arts, and to read as much as possible.    Her early favorites were fairy tales, and later the male authors of the Latin American "Boom," particularly Jorge Luis Borges, Manuel Puig, and Juan Rulfo.    More recently she has focused on women writers such as the Catalan author Merce Rodoreda, the American "working class" writer Pat Ellis Taylor, and the Chinese-American writer Maxine Hong Kingston.[272] She does not mention Mexican women writers as influences on her work, but there are obvious parallels with the themes and literary techniques of authors such as Elena Poniatowska, Brianda Domecq, Silvia Molina, and Angeles Mastretta.[273]    Sandra was assisted along the way by some of her creative writing teachers, by Gary Soto (who helped with *Bad Boys*), and by Nick Kanellos of Arte Público Press, who encouraged her to send him her stories.    She was prodded by her agent Susan Bergholz, who waited four years for Sandra to answer her messages, and then with a few stories finally in hand, Bergholz negotiated the lucrative contract with Random House for Sandra.

Sandra regrets not contacting Susan earlier, as well as not always focusing on her writing, or the topics of most interest to her. "Don't waste time," Sandra insists, when she's speaking to a group of students.[274]    She recommends that you only write about things for which you feel passion, and not waste time writing about anything else. Aspiring writers should try not to focus too much on publication, according to Sandra: "Publishing is the least important level of verification.... Writing is to get in touch with

272 Jussawalla 303.
273 See *Broken Bars: New Perspectives from Mexican Women Writers*, by Kay S. García.
274 OLLU website, OLLU Literary Festival 2011.

some intimate part of yourself. Publishing, fame, money, if you get it at all in your lifetime, is just icing on the cake but not the cake. Writing is a form of meditation."[275]

In her current project, *Writing in My Pajamas*, Sandra will be offering more detailed advice to writers. The title reflects a point she made in a lecture at OLLU: "Imagine you're sitting at a table in your pajamas, talking to someone who won't care that you're in your wrinkled pajamas—use that voice, at least for a first draft. You might want to fancy it up a bit later, but just to get something down on paper."[276] Sandra uses this image to get workshop participants to write with a natural voice, as if talking to a close friend and wearing something comfortable, rather than getting "dressed up in a suit" and pretending to be someone you're not. "Then once it's all done," she added in an interview, "revise as if your enemy were going to read it!"[277]

Sandra has used the pain and trauma in her life to work on spiritual growth and she has incorporated that awareness into her writing. "I have to be able to grow spiritually to be able to interpret and to guide. I find myself in the role of guiding a community."[278] One of her goals as a writer is to motivate people to participate in improving their world: "I have the power to make people think in a different way. It's a different way of defining power, and it is something that I don't want to abuse or lose," she has said.[279]

Although Sandra identifies herself as a feminist, her early feminism was delineated by her class, ethnicity, and experience in the *barrio*. As she has matured, she has widened the spectrum of her concerns to include people around the world:

---

275 Kevane 57.
276 "Author Sandra Cisneros explains 'Writing in my Pajamas.'"
277 Shea 5.
278 Kevane, 54.
279 Mirriam-Goldberg 7.

As I am getting older, I am writing more about global connections. How do I make people understand that the war in Bosnia is affecting them? How does one connect with a massacre in Rwanda or a woman raped by pirates in the Asiatic Sea? How does one connect the killings of people in Chiapas to a worker here in San Antonio? What is my role as a writer to the citizens of this country? That is what I am concerned about now.[280]

Sandra is one of the contemporary authors who has been most effective at using her writing as a means to encourage social progress, and she has supported other authors who are making a similar effort. She has combined her solitary literary work with public activism in a dynamic and inspirational way. With the exception of a brief stint as a visiting professor in Chico, California, she has kept her feet firmly planted in San Antonio, and has contributed not only to that community but also to cultural life in Texas. Although she still remembers what it was like to have pancakes and peanut butter for dinner, with scurrying rodents for company, she now lives in a place where she can dine on Mexican, Tex-Mex or any international cuisine she wishes, and she enjoys the company of her six dogs, four cats, and a parrot named Augustina. Her famously purple house at the edge of the San Antonio River is now Mexican pink, with a neon-green door, and in 2012 she put it up for sale without knowing where her next home would be. Wherever she goes, I am sure Sandra will be noticed and will make a difference in people's lives, whether she is writing about a lost cat, or about global connections.

§ § §

---

280 Kevane 53.

# Bibliography

## Books

Cisneros, Sandra. *Caramelo*. New York: Vintage Books, Random House, 2003.

---. *Have You Seen Marie?* New York: Alfred A. Knopf, 2012.

---. *Loose Woman*. New York: Alfred A. Knopf, 1994.

---. *My Wicked Wicked Ways*. New York: Alfred A. Knopf, 1995.

---. *The House on Mango Street*. 1984. New York: Alfred A. Knopf, 1994.

---. *Woman Hollering Creek and Other Stories*. New York: Random House, 1991.

Jago, Carol. *Sandra Cisneros in the Classroom*. Urbana, IL: National Council of Teachers of English, 2002.

Mirriam-Goldberg, Caryn. *Sandra Cisneros: Latina Writer and Activist*. Berkeley Heights, NJ: Enslow Publishers, 1998.

Rivera, Carmen. *Border Crossings and Beyond: The Life and Works of Sandra Cisneros*. 2009. eBook.

## Articles, Book Chapters; and Web Pages (web pages accessed Feb – Mar, 2013)

Allen, Paula. "Woman Hollering Creek's name evokes chilling explanations." *San Antonio Express-News*, 22 Feb 2004, 5H.

Aranda, Pilar E. Rodríguez. "On the Solitary Fate of Being Mexican, Female, Wicked and Thirty-three: An Interview with Writer Sandra Cisneros." *The Americas Review*. Vol. 18, No. 1, 64-80.

"Author Sandra Cisneros explains 'Writing in my Pajamas.'" 25 Feb 2010. http://youtube.com.

Badur, Diana I. *"Sandra Cisneros: 'La Gritona.'"* *Eureka Studies in Teaching Short Fiction*. Vol. 5, No. 1, Fall 2004, 137-139.

Barbato, Joseph. "Latino Writers in the American Market." *Publishers Weekly*. 01 Feb 1991, 17-21.

Benson, Sheila. "From the Barrio to the Brownstone." *Los Angeles Times*, May 7, 1991, F7.

Bruns, Roger. "Sandra Cisneros." *Icons of Latino America*, Vol. 1. Westport, Connecticut: Greenwood Press, 2008, 122-144.

Cisneros, Sandra. "Do You Know Me?: I wrote *The House on Mango Street*." *The Americas Review*, Volume 15, Issue 1, spring 1987, 77-79.

---. "Foreword." *Holler If You Hear Me: The Education of a Teacher and His Students*. Michie, Gregory. New York: Teachers College Press, 1999.

---. "Ghosts and Voices: Writing from Obsession." *The Americas Review*. Volume 15, Issue 1, spring 1987, 69-73.

---. "Notes to a Younger Writer." *The Americas Review*. Volume 15, Issue 1, spring 1987, 74-76.

---. Website: http://sandracisneros.com.

Dasenbrock, Reed Way. "Sandra Cisneros." *Interviews with Writers of the Post-Colonial World*. Feroza Jussawalla and Reed Way

Dasenbrock. Jackson & London: University Press of Mississippi, 1992, 286-306.

Gass-Poore, Jordan. "Q & A with Sandra Cisneros." *The University Star.* 13 Oct 2010, http://star.txstate.edu.

Juffer, Jane. "Sandra Cisneros' Career." Modern American Poetry Website. http://www.english.illinois.edu.

Kevane, Bridget and Juanita Heredia. "A Home in the Heart: An Interview with Sandra Cisneros." *Latina Self-Portraits: Interviews With Contemporary Women Writers.* Kevane and Heredia. Albuquerque: University of New Mexico Press, 2000, 45-57.

Lowery, George. "Cisneros tries to make peace with the creative process." *Chronicle Online.* 17 Sep 2007. http://www.chronicleonline.com.

Macías, Francisco. "Sandra Cisneros Discusses Fairy Tales, Where She Likes to Read." *The Huffington Post.* 02 Nov 2012, http://www.huffingtonpost.com.

McCracken, Ellen. "Sandra Cisneros." *Latino and Latina Writers.* Alan West. New York: Charles Scribner's Sons, 2004, 229-249.

Navarro, Mireya. "Telling a Tale of Immigrants Whose Stories Go Untold." *The New York Times.* 12 Nov 2002, E1 and E7.

Sagel, Jim. "Sandra Cisneros: conveying the riches of the Latin American culture is the author's literary goal." *Publishers Weekly.* 238.15, 29 Mar 1991, 74.

"Sandra Cisneros: Community Activism." 5 Mar 2009. http://www.youtube.com.

"Sandra Cisneros: I Hate the Iowa Writer's Workshop." 23 Apr 2009. http://www.youtube.com.

Shea, Renée H. "Sandra Cisneros: Interview by Renée H. Shea." *The Bookwoman,* Issue 60, Winter 1997, 1-5.

Tabor, Mary B.W. "At The Library With: Sandra Cisneros; A Solo Traveler In Two Worlds." *The New York Times*. 07 Jan 1993, http://www.nytimes.com.

Vidimos, Robin. "Antidote for climate of fear: Complicated 'Caramelo' has some challenging ideas." *The Denver Post*. 27 Mar 2005, F-09.

# Chapter Six
# Multiple Voices of Activism

"As you discover what strength you can draw from your community in this world from which it stands apart, look outward as well as inward. Build bridges instead of walls."

--Sonia Sotomayor

There are many ways to make a difference in this world, from the local to the international level and in almost every arena or profession. What we need is true interconnection and solidarity with others, in a world that is increasingly linked together by electronic information but not by human collectivity. As long as one group of people is oppressed for any reason, we are all diminished. The previous chapters portray a few leaders who have transcended individualism and have established important connections to other people and organizations in order to improve the society in which we live. Their life stories have been told in detail so that the readers can imagine –if only for a brief time— what it feels like to be those people, to live their lives, think their thoughts, face their challenges, overcome those obstacles, and manage to help others succeed, too. Thus, their stories provide a few pieces of an intricate puzzle.

This chapter presents a wide variety of Latinos in different fields who are using their skills, resources, and prestige to influence our society in positive ways. I have included examples of individuals and organizations that are operating on the local, state, national and international levels. However, the sections are not organized by level, but rather by fields of expertise, which include 1) Politicians 2) Leaders in Education 3) Community Outreach, Leadership Training, and Labor Organizing (grouped together because they overlap), and 4) Author-activists. A few more fields and representative people will be mentioned in the Conclusion to this book.

These brief portraits will provide many more pieces of the global picture, and will suggest others, so that the reader may perceive the complex tapestry of people working toward goals that sometimes benefit a specific group of people, but that ultimately benefit all of society. Such progress could be even more significant if we all followed the principle of Dolores Huerta's "Weaving Movements" initiative, and cooperated with each other. Ideally, we could go beyond alliances of convenience, and truly commit to other causes as our own.

The sections in this chapter are of various lengths because they include only the details that are most relevant to the themes of this book, and some personal stories that are particularly poignant or representative of many people's experiences. For every individual portrayed in this chapter, there are countless more who are not mentioned. Choosing among so many dedicated advocates was extremely difficult, but the upside was discovering hundreds of Latino activists who are striving to improve the lives of others. I tip my hat to all of those who should have been included.

# Politicians

Politicians provide good examples of people who have learned to form coalitions among many different interest groups in order to further a progressive agenda. An impressive number of Latino politicians are gaining a national reputation. I have chosen to highlight three representative politicians who have risen from humble beginnings, have overcome adversity, and are notable for their advocacy for immigration reform, gay rights, and other progressive issues. At the end of this section, I have included information about one conservative politician who has supported immigration reform, and could be an important ally for advocates of such reform.

### Julián Castro, Mayor of San Antonio

The national spotlight was turned on Julián Castro, the 37-year-old mayor of San Antonio, when he became the first Latino ever to deliver a Keynote Address at the Democratic National Convention, in September 2012. There has been widespread speculation that he will be the first Latino president of the United States. One can see obvious parallels in the lives of Barack Obama and Julián Castro: both were raised by single mothers, earned law degrees from Harvard, and have based their politics on issues rather than on race. As mayor, Julián Castro has focused on creating jobs and promoting educational opportunities. He managed to get a sales tax increase approved in order to finance pre-school education for low-income children, and he has supported efforts to increase literacy, reduce the drop-out rate, and establish a resource center for students applying for college. Like Sonia Sotomayor, he is an outspoken advocate for Affirmative Action, which he credits for giving him the opportunity to attend Stanford University as an undergraduate. He is a pragmatist who supports free trade, a balanced budget, and an eclectic energy policy that includes the use of fossil fuels, but he has served as grand marshal of the gay rights parade in San Antonio, and he is pro-choice. He has championed the cause of immigration reform, calling the proposed changes both pro-family and pro-business. "It's the right thing to do, and it's in our nation's and our economy's best interests.... America is watching, Washington. It's time to get this done," he wrote.[281]

Julián Castro has been described as "cerebral, serious, self-contained and highly efficient....Nothing seems to ruffle him."[282] This is something else he has in common with "No Drama Obama." He learned from his defeat the first time he ran for mayor in 2005, and during the next campaign he did better at reaching out to more of his constituents. "It's true that defeat is a better teacher than victory," he admitted, "you have to think about what you could have done better. I took time after the [first race for mayor] to do that, and I set about creating a broader coalition of support."[283] Subsequently, he ran a successful campaign for mayor in 2009 and chose to pursue a second term in 2013, in spite of being pressured to run for governor. As mayor, he has made an effort to represent people of all backgrounds. "The great cities of the world are not defined by one or two minorities, religions, or backgrounds," he stated. "It must be that way for San Antonio as well."[284] At the Democratic National Convention he goaded

281 Castro. "Hey Congress: Get immigration reform done."
282 Chavets 1/11 and 3/11. (Numbers after articles found online indicate the page number on the print-out/total number of pages, as a general indication of where to find the information in the article.)
283 Smith 1/4.
284 Ibid.

everybody to contribute to social progress when he declared: "Our responsibility is to come together as one nation, one community, to ensure opportunity for our children.... It begins with you, it begins now."[285]

Although he does not focus exclusively on Latino issues, Julián Castro maintains contact with the Latino community, he is working on improving his Spanish, and he often pays tribute to his mother, Rosie Castro, who was one of the leaders of the Chicano political party *La Raza Unida*. His twin brother, Joaquín Castro, was a representative in the Texas legislature from 2003 to 2013, and currently he represents Texas in the U.S. House of Representatives. Their political success does not appear to have gone to their heads. In 2010 Joaquín told a reporter: "Julián and I are just two guys from the bad side of San Antonio."[286]

## Nydia M. Velázquez, Representative for New York

Another politician who has embraced a variety of causes is Nydia M. Velázquez, the first Puerto Rican woman elected to the U.S. House of Representatives. She has represented first the 12th District and then the redistributed 7th District of New York since 1992, and has been reelected ten times. When the boundaries

---

285 Castro. Keynote speech at Democratic National Convention.
286 Chavets 10/11.

were redrawn to include fewer Latinos in her district, there was speculation that Nydia Veláquez might lose the next election. Her continuing success could be attributed to her ability to forge alliances with and represent the interests of constituents from a variety of backgrounds.

Nydia Velázquez was born in 1953 in Yabucoa, Puerto Rico, as one of nine children, and she became the first person in her family to earn a college degree. After earning a master's degree while on scholarship at New York University, she taught Puerto Rican studies at Hunter College in New York for several years. Nydia entered the political arena when she became the first Latina to serve on the New York City Council. In 1986 she became the Director of the U.S. Department of Puerto Rican Community Affairs, where she began a very successful Latino empowerment program called *"Atrévete"* (Dare to do it).

While in Congress, Nydia Velázquez has defended the rights of undocumented immigrants, and she has spoken at demonstrations to promote immigration reform, in which she has used Dolores Huerta's rallying cry, *Sí se puede* (Yes we can). She has been a significant voice on issues relating to Puerto Rico, and has promoted the right of Puerto Ricans on the island to determine the form of their own government. She once favored independence, then switched to supporting the Commonwealth (the status quo in 2013), but she has stated that she will support whatever the people of Puerto Rico choose in a federally-sponsored plebiscite. In 2006 she became the first Latina to chair a full Congressional committee when she was appointed Chairwoman of the House Small Business Committee. On this committee she has promoted minority-owned and woman-owned businesses, and she prompted an investigation into small business loans being given to divisions of large firms.

Nydia Velázlquez has tried to improve the lives of the working class and poor families by fighting for affordable, high-quality housing, education and health care for everybody. She has defended the rights of all people to be protected against domestic abuse, regardless of legal status or sexual orientation. During debate in Congress before the passage of the 2013 Violence Against Women Act, Nydia Velázquez spoke against the Republican amendment that would have denied protection to undocumented workers and members of the LGBTQ community. Her speech contributed to a positive outcome: the bill was approved without the discriminatory amendment.[287]

Videos of Nydia Velázquez's speeches reveal that she is confident, wise and articulate. Her energetic but measured style contrasts with the fiery orator, Luis Gutiérrez, who is also in his eleventh term in the U.S. House of Representatives.

## Luis Gutiérrez, Representative for Illinois

A 2010 Pew Hispanic Center national survey rated Luis Gutiérrez the number two most influential Latino leader in the United States, second only to Justice Sonia Sotomayor. He is known for his zealous advocacy of immigration reform and his confrontational attitude. He has been criticized for "badgering" the President on the issue:

---

287 Information in this paragraph comes from Nydia M. Velázquez's website and the NYTimes article "Nydia M. Velazquez."

"Gutiérrez… is the most passionate, tireless, and nettlesome voice in Congress on immigration matters. He's a constant presence at rallies and on TV, defending the undocumented and railing against xenophobia."[288] Like Dolores Huerta, he is courageous and willing to participate in acts of nonviolent civil disobedience; in 2010 he was arrested at an immigration protest in front of the White House. When asked why he participates in such protests, he said, "We cannot be a slave to the legislative process. That's what we've done, and it hasn't served us very well."[289]

Luis Gutiérrez was born in Chicago in 1953. His mother was a factory worker and his father drove a taxi. When he was in high school his family moved to his parents' hometown of San Sebastián, Puerto Rico, where he struggled to learn Spanish and to understand his bicultural identity. He endured the same pain and confusion that Sandra Cisneros describes when she writes about her early visits to Mexico. He returned to Chicago to enroll at Northeastern Illinois University, where he earned a degree in English. He worked as a cab driver, teacher, and social worker before being elected to the City Council in 1986. He married his high school sweetheart and he and his wife have been married for over thirty years, with two children and one grandchild. In 1992 he became the first Latino to be elected to Congress from the Midwest and he has been reelected ever since.[290]

In order to make a point, Luis Gutiérrez sometimes uses sarcastic humor. In a scene that could have played out well on Saturday Night Live, he presented a game called "Pick out the Immigrant" to members of Congress. As playful-but-stinging criticism of Arizona's "papers please" policy (which allows officers of the law to request identification from people who look like

288 Campo-Flores 1/3.
289 Ibid. 2-3/3.
290 Unless otherwise noted, information on Luis Gutiérrez comes from the Politico website, and/or from Luis Gutiérrez's website.

undocumented immigrants), he held up pairs of enlarged photos and challenged the representatives to test their abilities. "Can you pick the immigrant?" he asked. "I can't, because I'm not a trained Arizona State Trooper." He then referred to notes to reveal which ones were immigrants, since they all were from Europe or Canada and apparently could not be easily identified. All of the citizens, of course, had dark eyes, black hair, and names like Geraldo Rivera and Sonia Sotomayor.

Even though his adversarial methods have been effective, Luis Gutiérrez realizes that proponents of immigration reform need to reach out to everybody who might be an ally in order to make significant progress. When he addressed immigrants in Denver in February 2013, he urged them to reach out to Republicans. "There are good people in the Republican Party who want to help us," he insisted. Then he suggested that the immigrants tell their stories to the Republican politicians and ask for their support.[291]

Luis Gutiérrez has declared that his one loyalty is to the immigrant community, but his political history and voting record indicate his strong support for many progressive causes, including workers' rights, LGBTQ rights, women's rights, consumer protection, veterans' benefits, and efforts to improve communities. As the senior member of the Financial Services Committee, he has worked toward including more minorities in the banking system and improving lending regulations. As an Alderman in Chicago, he worked on improving the Mass Transit system, affordable housing, and a law to ban discrimination based on sexual orientation. He has supported independence for Puerto Rico, and has defended the *Vieques* protest movement, which resulted in the closure of the U.S. naval training range in Puerto Rico.

---

291 "Luis Gutiérrez Tells Denver Immigrants…"

## Marco Rubio, Senator for Florida

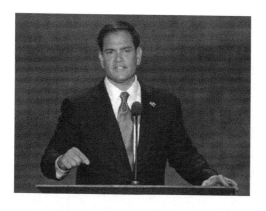

Any search for Republican allies would have to include Senator Marco Rubio of Florida, who is another politician with a realistic shot at becoming the first Latino president of the United States. He made a valiant effort to transcend partisan politics in 2013 when he proposed a conservative version of immigration reform. He took the lead on the bi-partisan congressional committee dubbed "the Gang of Eight," and the bill they drafted was subsequently passed by the Senate. Marco Rubio has both personal and political reasons for taking this stand. His parents are Cuban immigrants, his wife's parents are Colombian immigrants, he lives in a neighborhood consisting mainly of immigrants, and his mother has pressured him to pay attention to the immigrants' call for reform. Politically, it would be to his advantage in a future presidential election if he managed to get his plan approved by Congress and thereby win back some Latino voters for the GOP.[292]

---

292 In this section on Marco Rubio, the political information comes mainly from his speeches and from articles in *Time* and *The New York Times*, while the biographical information comes mainly from his memoir and his website. Since most of this information comes from multiple sources, I have noted only the direct quotes.

In an effort to escape the poverty into which they were born, Marco Rubio's parents left Cuba in 1956, during the time of Fulgencio Batista's dictatorship. They found work in a series of low-paying jobs, but managed to raise four children who all graduated from college. In his memoir, *An American Son*, Marco Rubio pays tribute to his parents and to other family members who have made significant sacrifices in order to make his political success possible.

Marco Rubio was born in Miami, Florida in 1971 and has spent most of his life there, with the exception of a few years in Las Vegas as a child. He played football in high school and was good enough to earn a scholarship to Tarkio College in Missouri, where he studied for one year before transferring to the University of Florida. He completed his bachelor's degree in 1993, and three years later he received a law degree from the University of Miami. He launched his political career in 1998 when he won a seat on the West Miami City Commission. He served in the Florida House of Representatives from 2000 to 2008, and became a U.S. senator in 2010.

Just three years after arriving in Washington, he was hailed as "the most influential voice in the national debate over immigration reform" by Michael Grunwald of *Time* magazine, who specified that "his impeccably nuanced positions have become the core of the Senate plan."[293] The bill passed by the Senate in June 2013 would provide a 13-year path to citizenship for the eleven million undocumented immigrants in the United States, but that process would take longer and be more complicated than most immigration advocates had hoped. The bill called for an additional twenty thousand border patrol agents and seven hundred more miles of fencing along the border. It would not honor same-sex

See the Bibliography for details on these sources.
293 Grunwald 26 and 29.

marriages, and would not extend health care benefits to newly documented immigrants. Even with these provisions, the House of Representatives declined to discuss this bill, and chose to draft a separate bill.

In a country that is so evenly divided, there are times when coalitions or alliances must be formed around a single issue in order to make some progress, and sometimes conservative reform can serve as an important step toward more progressive reform. However, most advocates of immigration reform agree that it is important to continue working toward a more comprehensive reform that is not predicated on the increased militarization of the U.S.-Mexico border.

# Leaders in Education

Significant improvements are being made at all levels of education in order to prepare students for a more inclusive world, and inspire them to work for positive social change. In this section I will present the ideas of three Latino leaders in education: an associate dean at a university, the executive director of a statewide coalition, and the president of a national association of Hispanic colleges and universities. Each of these leaders has built on the work of many colleagues who came before them, or who have worked alongside them toward a common goal.

# Latino and Latina Leaders

## Susana Rivera-Mills,
## Founder of Center for Latin@ Studies and Engagement

Susana[294] was only eight years old when the civil war in El Salvador began to encroach upon her secure, upper-middle class existence. By the time she was twelve, the constant threat of violence had reached such an extreme level that it was necessary for her to flee the capital city of San Salvador on a dark night, huddled with her younger brother in the back seat of the family car.[295] Overnight they became immigrants in a strange land, taking refuge with a relative in San Francisco. Susana's parents found minimum-wage jobs at a nursery and she worked side by side with them on weekends and summers. She could have dead-ended there, eking out an existence by laboring in the fields, up to her

---

294 As in previous chapters, I ask for the understanding of the people portrayed in this chapter as well as the reader in regard to the use of first names. I have chosen to use first names in the longer sections because I wish to help the reader identify with these leaders.

295 For this section I have combined information from several long conversations that I had with Susana in 2012 and 2013, as well as from the article by Lee Sherman (see bibliography).

knees in mud, but thanks to her parents' work ethic and two Latino teachers who recognized her potential, she was encouraged to study hard and go on to college.

While still in high school she attained a third-degree black belt in karate and explored a wide variety of spiritual beliefs. Susana credits her involvement with martial arts and her individual spiritual quest, as well as her parents' and teachers' influence, for her ability to succeed. Because of that support system, she managed to transform her personal struggle into a lifelong commitment to creating a place of belonging for Latinos in the United States. A turning point came for her when she was inspired by the poetry of Julia Alvarez,[296] whose verses about life as an immigrant helped Susana realize that she was not the only one struggling to fit in, and that she could choose the direction of her own life. This anecdote highlights the importance of immigrants' telling their own stories, as was mentioned in the chapters on Jorge Ramos and Sandra Cisneros.

Susana believes that experiencing the freedom to make choices can be transformational. According to her, it is essential for schools to create safe spaces that allow students to explore options and make choices about the learning that they are doing, because that is part of the empowerment process. They need to learn that "one choice versus the other leads to one set of consequences versus the other."[297] Making the right choices has contributed to Susana's completion of a Ph.D. in sociolinguistics, and to her becoming a professor of Spanish and subsequently the associate dean of the

---

296 Julia Alvarez was raised in the Dominican Republic and New York City. She writes poetry, essays, and novels, and is best known for her works *How the García Girls Lost Their Accent* and *In the Time of the Butterflies.*
297 García, Kay. "Interview with Susana Rivera-Mills." All quotes in this section on Susana are from this interview, unless otherwise noted.

College of Liberal Arts at Oregon State University (OSU). She also chose to lead an interdisciplinary group of colleagues in their efforts to establish an innovative support center at OSU for Latino students and researchers, called the Center for Latin@ Studies and Engagement (CL@SE)[298], and to serve as its transitional director.

In addition to helping students navigate the daunting university system, CL@SE encourages engaged research, a transformative type of study that involves making connections with Latino communities and determining what kind of research might be most beneficial to them. For example, Susana has studied different Latino communities in both the southwest and Oregon, analyzing variables such as age of arrival in the United States and educational attainment, in order to understand what determines whether Latinos retain their language and cultural identity as they adjust to new lives in this country. She has discovered that members of a particular community in Independence, Oregon, continue to maintain fluency in Spanish for five or six generations, well beyond the norm of three generations of linguistic preservation. According to Lee Sherman, "She attributes this robust language retention in part to Independence's deeply rooted Latino heritage, passed down … by hard-working, close-knit, tradition-loving families."[299]

The purpose of engaged research is to further the understanding of Latino (and other) communities. According to Susana, "It's not a one-way street. It's a partnership between academia and the community to create shared knowledge. You give the community your ear and listen, listen, listen."[300] Being able to listen intensely, a skill Susana calls "profound listening," is essential for engaging the "other" (anyone who is different from oneself). "You can't really listen to someone genuinely if you're not interested in what

298 The term Latin@ is another way to say "Latino and Latina," and thus it includes both males and females.
299 Sherman 24.
300 Quoted in Sherman 25.

they're about to say," explains Susana. "You can't be jumping to conclusions or thinking about what you want to answer. You have to rid yourself of biases that you are aware of and put aside things that may prevent you from truly knowing a human being."

Susana prefers to interact with people informally, and to identify herself simply as Susana, eschewing all roles, titles, or ethnicities, and simply talking with the person, human to human. If you identify someone with a certain label, according to her, you have an expectation as to what that person brings to the table. She believes that intellectual curiosity is important. "You have to look at every interaction as an opportunity to learn more about somebody else's life experience," she declares. "That's how we engage and build a social relationship." When it's possible, Susana likes to connect with people on a spiritual level, even though it's very rare to find someone else who has integrated their spirituality into their whole life. "So many of us divide life into categories," she says, "and these categories are damaging because you constantly have to tear yourself into different pieces. [I am pleased] whenever I meet somebody who can actually live a whole life and be who they are no matter where they go."

"I want the message to be exactly the same, no matter where I'm speaking," declares Susana. "Integrity is tied to consistency, so I try to express the same opinion about issues regardless of the audience or the context. That way people know what I stand for, and if they put me on a committee, they know what message to expect." According to Susana, there is an important connection between spirituality and leadership. A leader's integrity, ethics, and decision-making skills are often tested, so it is important to know what your core values are. "I can't imagine being a leader without first finding out well what my own personal values are, what grounds me, what propels me to do what I do. It's my understanding of my purpose for why I am here."

One of the things that Susana has learned from being in a leadership position is that the voices of grassroots movements —as expressed in demonstrations, rallies, and strikes— often stop at the steps of the capitol or the doors of administration buildings. Since she is privileged to have a position on the inside, she tries to use her voice to amplify the voices on the outside, or even better, to find ways to allow them to speak for themselves. If she can bring members of a particular group to a meeting, she prefers to do that. "If we can create a web of allies between our grassroots movements, community leaders, politicians, educators, and other leaders, then we will have a very solid structure that can approach an issue from different levels, where the voices are not left outside but are echoed at every level, within every wall, inside these institutions."

"Education is really the only revolution that's sustainable, that lasts and that actually can have an impact, an influence on positive change that is long term," according to Susana. She was a contributing editor of a collection of essays that present innovative pedagogical methods for establishing connections with underrepresented communities: *Building Communities and Making Connections in the 21st Century.* These essays provide examples of how students are being prepared for an increasingly global society by establishing alliances with communities and by performing service as part of their coursework. For a more detailed discussion of this book and a description of innovative methodology, please refer to the Appendix entitled "Transformative Education."

**Eduardo Angulo,**
**Director of Salem-Keizer Coalition for Equality**

Eduardo Angulo is the executive director and co-founder of the Salem-Keizer Coalition for Equality (SKCE) in Salem, Oregon, and a member of the steering committee of the Oregon Alliance for Education Equity (OAEE). Consequently, he provides a good example of what can be accomplished by someone working at the state level. He is originally from Puerto Rico, but has lived in Oregon for many years. He attended Linfield College in McMinnville, Oregon, and has been involved in community organizing in this state since 1994.[301] He is a strong advocate for public education reform, and has presented before school boards and state agencies, published online articles and reports, and has been interviewed by the SKCE film group about the goals of his organization. Although he is an enthusiastic supporter of the Latino community, he always includes other minorities in his advocacy, and makes a point of naming them in his reports and speeches. "We are saying that the status quo doesn't work for students of color," he declared in an interview. "We are going to help the school district, because we know our communities and we know our kids, so we are going

301 Unless otherwise noted, information on Eduardo Angulo comes from the SKCE website.

to help you create a curriculum that will help you reach out to parents... and bring out the best in our kids."[302]

In an online editorial, he states, "Historically our children and youth of color and English Language Learners have not been served well by our public education system as the achievement gap remains steady after ten years of the [No Child Left Behind][303] national law.... I encourage all our supporters and allies to be part of the solution by getting engaged [in the process of reform]."[304] He calls for collective active involvement, in which community leaders provide workshops for parents, then parents train other parents; and communities sponsor youth programs, then older participants serve as role models for younger children.[305] The SKCE's vision of fostering mutual accountability between children, parents and schools is shared by the Oregon Alliance for Education Equity, which is a non-partisan coalition with 17 member organizations, supported in principle by an additional 16 groups.

Eduardo Angulo represented this sizable alliance before the Oregon Education Investment Board, providing specific recommendations for education reform. He called for holding all elected and appointed education leaders accountable for improving the success rate of students of color, addressing the inequities in student discipline rate, and improving on methods of collecting and reporting data. "We must look at the impact [of educational policies] on all students and the specific, and almost

---

302 "Eduardo Angulo Before Salem-Keizer School Board Meeting."
303 No Child Left Behind is a federal law enacted in 2001 that requires states to develop assessments in basic skills and give these assessments to all students at select grade levels in order to receive federal school funding.
304 Angulo, "Change is in the air..." 1/2.
305 Ibid. 2/2 and "Eduardo Angulo Before Salem-Keizer School Board Meeting."

always different, impact on subgroups of students," he testified.[306] Furthermore, he advocated for including parents and community members in the process of establishing educational goals.

The mission of the Oregon Alliance for Education Equity is "to eliminate racial and ethnic disparities in education and ensure that students of color and students learning English graduate from high school prepared to be successful adults and global citizens."[307] Because it unites so many different organizations, the OAEE is a good illustration of how to make connections and create solidarity across differences in order to promote positive social change.

### Antonio R. Flores, President of Hispanic Association of Colleges and Universities

On the national level, Antonio R. Flores is creating a web of alliances as president of the Hispanic Association of Colleges and Universities (HACU), an organization that represents more than 400 colleges and universities throughout the country. HACU has helped

---

306 Angulo, "Update from the Oregon Alliance for Education Equity (OAEE)," 1/4.
307 "Oregon Alliance for Education Equity (OAEE) press release."

thousands of Latino students by providing college preparation and retention programs, along with internships, scholarships, and career development opportunities. During the first 16 years of Antonio Flores' leadership, he coordinated the distribution of more than $1.7 billion in federal funding while providing financial and programmatic oversight to institutions with a minimum of 25 percent Latino student enrollment.[308] In an article on influential Latinos, Laura Rivas comments, "Anyone positioned to improve the quality of education for Latinos is critical, and through HACU, Flores holds colleges and universities accountable to their Latino Students."[309]

During his tenure, Antonio Flores has greatly increased the size and scope of his organization by creating new categories of membership to accommodate universities with less than 25 percent Latino enrollment, as well as Latino-serving school districts. He has expanded the association internationally by creating affiliations with at least 48 institutions located in Latin America and Europe. In an interview at an international conference in Ecuador, Antonio Flores highlighted the importance of promoting more student exchanges between universities in Latin America and those in North America. In addition, he declared that at the K-12 level we need to do more to help Latino students prepare for college studies, and at the university level we need to include more courses on the languages and cultures of Latin America.[310]

Antonio Flores has been a strong advocate for immigration reform, particularly as it relates to education. In a speech at the DREAM Act Summit (a conference to promote the Development, Relief, and Education for Alien Minors Act), he spoke in support of

308 Unless otherwise noted, all information on Antonio Flores and the HACU comes from the Hispanic Association of Colleges and Universities website.
309 Rivas (no page number).
310 "Entrevista Dr. Antonio Flores."

the "best and the brightest" Latino students who wish to go on to college, referring to them as "model citizens without citizenship," and calling on politicians to act as quickly as possible, in a bi-partisan manner. "Mr. President and members of Congress," he concluded, "it is high time for you to act on the dream."[311]

Having completed two undergraduate degrees in Mexico, a master's degree and a doctorate in higher education administration from the University of Michigan-Ann Arbor, Antonio Flores prepared himself well for the demands of his chosen profession. He has been honored with a long list of honorary doctorates and awards, including lifetime achievement awards from the Educational Policy Institute and *Hispanic Business* magazine. He serves as a role model for young Latinos, and as an example of what can be achieved on the national and international levels through the creation of multiple connections and collaborations.

## Community Outreach, Leadership Training, Labor Organization

Just as educational institutions have incorporated feedback from communities, so have community outreach programs utilized schools and universities to inform and enhance their services. These connections have proven to be very rewarding. An excellent example of this trend is a former professor, Erlinda Gonzales-Berry, who founded the non-profit community organization Casa Latinos Unidos de Benton County, which operates on the local level, but has connections throughout the state of Oregon. Larry Kleinman is an example of a non-Latino ally who has been very active on the state level in all three of the fields represented in this section, while Juan Andrade Jr. provides a model for connecting leadership training with education at the national level.

---

311 "Antonio R. Flores speaks at DREAM Act Summit."

**Erlinda Gonzales-Berry,
Director of Casa Latinos Unidos**

Erlinda Gonzales-Berry was born in 1942 on a ranch outside Roy, a small rural community in northern New Mexico.[312] Her tranquil, secure existence came to an abrupt halt when a severe drought made it necessary for her family to move to Rosebud, New Mexico, where her mother found employment as the teacher in a one-room school. According to Teresa Márquez, "[Erlinda's] extended family of cousins, aunts, and uncles helped her cope with the racist remarks made against her and her family after the relocation."[313] Erlinda soon found herself serving as a teacher's aide to her mother, who encouraged her to pursue her studies.

After earning an undergraduate degree, a master's and a Ph.D.

312 Information in this section on Erlinda comes from my conversations with her as well as from the article written by Teresa Márquez. Unless otherwise noted, all of the quotes in this section are from an interview that I did with her on 25 April 2013.
313 Márquez 181.

from the University of New Mexico (UNM), Erlinda taught college courses elsewhere for several years and then returned to teach Spanish at UNM. There she created a program for students who spoke Spanish at home, fostering an appreciation of their own culture while formalizing their linguistic knowledge. In 1992 Erlinda became chair of the Spanish department at UNM, and five years later she was hired at Oregon State University to be chair of the newly formed Ethnic Studies Department. She worked at developing that department until 2007, when she retired from the university but not from public service.

Erlinda has written and/or edited several collections of essays, and has published a bilingual edition of her novel *Paletitas de guayaba/On a Train Called Absence* (2010). The Spanish version of this work was published in 1991, at the time when Sandra Cisneros' writing was breaking new ground for Latina authors in the mainstream English-language presses. Erlinda's novel is the story of a young Chicana student who travels to Mexico in an effort to understand her historical and mythical past as well as her complex, multicultural present. This work draws upon memories of a year spent with her family in Guadalajara, Mexico, where her father was working with the U.S. government to help eradicate hoof and mouth disease in cattle. The central themes of *Paletitas de guayaba* are the struggle to define a hybrid identity and the rebellion against sexism and racism. Although there might not have been any direct influence, these themes are echoed in many other works by Latinas, including Sandra Cisneros' book *Caramelo*, which was published a decade later.

Erlinda collaborated with Marcela Mendoza on *Mexicanos in Oregon*, a collection of essays and personal stories as told by people of Mexican descent who live in Oregon. In this work, once again, Erlinda tackles the difficult subject of the tension between two cultural realities. After referring to Américo Paredes' definition of a border as a sensitized area where two cultures or two political systems confront each other, the authors of this collection define the border for *mexicanos* in Oregon as "a socio-spatial line that mediates between the reality of their lives at home and that of the public space of mainstream culture. Thus, it is more intensely personal and psychological and it functions as a reminder of their isolation and of their separation from the dominant society."[314] Besides criticizing Oregon's unsavory history of discrimination against minority groups, Erlinda Gonzales-Berry and Marcela Mendoza highlight some of the contributions made by *mexicanos* to the state of Oregon. In the conclusion to their book, they underscore the importance of providing educational and economic opportunities for Latino children and families.

These issues and others raised by Erlinda during her academic career are now being addressed in a practical manner at Casa Latinos Unidos de Benton County (CLUBC). Erlinda maintains valuable connections with the university. Professors have collaborated with her on projects, and have sent her students to work as volunteers or interns. The twofold mission of CLUBC is to help Latinos learn the skills necessary for successful integration into the social and economic network of the area, and to create bridges with the broader community in order to make it easier for others to understand and appreciate Latino issues.

Erlinda has worked hard to create partnerships with other agencies. For example, she teamed up with the Salem-Keizer Coalition of Equality (based in Salem, Oregon) to address the "achievement gap," the issue of Latino students lagging behind other students' achievement levels. She has used SKCE materials to offer workshops for Latino parents in an effort to enhance parental involvement with the educational process. CLUBC has

314 Gonzales-Berry and Marcela Mendoza 14.

collaborated with the Benton County Health Department, the social justice group at a local church, the Rural Organizing Project, and *Causa*, a statewide organization for promoting immigrants' rights. Erlinda and other CLUBC staff members have joined with many Latino organizations to help organize and participate in the annual May Day march in Salem, Oregon, to support immigrants' and workers' rights.

In order to reach out to the non-Latino community, CLUBC has offered workshops on immigration and sponsored cultural events that celebrate Latino culture. Erlinda and her staff held a community forum to report on their educational assessment project, which illustrates the need for equal access to education. They have given presentations to teachers, school boards, and the executive council of the school district in order to address educational issues that affect Latinos and other minorities. "We take our mission of reaching out to non-Latinos seriously," declares Erlinda, "because Latinos, especially immigrants, will not be able to integrate until the mainstream community opens itself up, and in order to do that we need to create the bridges and do the educational work."

CLUBC not only communicates Latino needs, but also provides a window into the Latino community and their many contributions to society. Erlinda explains that Latinos have contributed to the creation of wealth in this country, through their labor in a wide variety of industries, such as mining, railroads, cattle-raising, and agriculture. She also mentions their contributions to popular culture: their influence can be seen in art, music, movies, and many other aspects of life in the U.S. Moreover, according to Erlinda, they have contributed to family values in this country, providing a broader definition of family and emphasizing the importance of family unity. Families gather to support one another, and to celebrate life. "The notion that life is to be enjoyed," she observes, "is perhaps an even more valuable contribution, something that has not been fully embraced by U.S. society. You share life with others, and enjoy the experience. In Spanish we use the term *convivencia*, or living with others."

Social events can provide opportunities to interact with the "other." Erlinda mentions that sharing food, especially in someone's home, is a good way to get past cultural barriers and develop friendships. Erlinda believes that creating solidarity across differences is an important goal, but first Latinos need to feel empowered and comfortable within their own cultural and linguistic milieu, and then they can move more easily across boundaries and work toward justice for all people. "Once they feel secure within their own community," she explains, "then a lot of things fall into place for them and they begin to see their personal struggles with a broader perspective." As an example of this, she mentions *Causa*, the statewide organization for immigration rights, which began working with the LGBTQ alliance on a particular issue. "Their joint effort initiated a felicitous collaboration and they've been working together ever since, and that's the way it should be," she concludes. Like Susana Rivera-Mills, Erlinda recognizes that there is a connection between spirituality and her work, even though she did not initiate her organization with that in mind. She believes that directing CLUBC has been the most satisfying work that she has ever done. "It's definitely spiritual work," she declares, "because it feeds my soul."

**Larry Kleinman,
Secretary-Treasurer of a Farmworkers Union**

Another person doing satisfying work is Larry Kleinman, secretary-treasurer of a farmworkers union (PCUN) and chair of the board of CAPACES Leadership Institute, both in Oregon. He has made significant contributions to the Latino community throughout his entire adult life. However, he insists that he has gained more than he has given. "Most people find that to be an incredible statement, given how much effort I have put in," he asserts, "but there's no equal if you are a person who is value-driven in life, to be able to live out your values and put them into action and actually see things come of that. That's a rare privilege to be able to do that."[315]

CAPACES (which means "capable") is an umbrella association that facilitates cooperation among nine Latino organizations

---

315 "Interview with Larry Kleinman." Unless otherwise noted, all of the quotes in this section are from this interview that I did with him on 6 May 2013.

in Oregon (including PCUN) that promote civic engagement, education reform and improved living and working conditions for farmworkers, immigrants and women. The CAPACES Leadership Institute (CLI), based in Woodburn, Oregon, provides materials and workshops to help Latinos acquire the skills and political consciousness that are needed to lead and support social justice work. According to their mission statement, CLI-trained leaders are organizing and mobilizing thousands of young Latinos eligible to vote, and educating them to support progressive positions. In addition, they are contributing to the movement to establish collective bargaining for farmworkers throughout Oregon. "These two advances alone," CLI asserts, "will significantly close the gap between the Latinos' marginal political and labor power and their immense contributions as workers and consumers."[316]

*Pineros y Campesinos Unidos del Noroeste* (Northwest Treeplanters and Farmworkers United, known as PCUN) was founded in 1985 and since then has registered more than 5,000 members, making it the largest Latino organization in Oregon. Located in Woodburn, PCUN has organized boycotts, marches, and strikes that have led to collective bargaining agreements for agricultural workers. They have worked for regulation of pesticides, improved housing, Latino voter participation, and immigration reform. Their local radio station KPCN-LP, supported by volunteers, attracts a large number of Latino listeners in the area. Their club called "*PCUNcitos* (little members of PCUN)" cultivates leadership in middle school students.[317] "PCUN has put the issue of justice for farmworkers on the map in Oregon," according to Peter S. Nicholson, "and everyone from the governor on down is taking notice."[318]

---

316 CAPACES website.
317 All information on PCUN up to this point in this paragraph comes from the PCUN website.
318 Nicholson 4/4.

## Kay (Kayla) S. García

Larry Kleinman has been involved in PCUN since before the beginning. In 1977 he helped establish the precursor to PCUN, the Willamette Valley Immigration Project, which provided legal advice and other services to undocumented workers. Finding inspiration in Cesar Chávez and Dolores Huerta's United Farmworkers Union, Larry and other leaders decided to form a union for farmworkers and treeplanters in Oregon. Currently, Larry is the only non-Latino on the 11-member board of directors for PCUN, and at first glance, he would seem to be an unlikely leader in a Latino organization. His grandparents were Russian Jews who immigrated to the United States after World War I, and Larry was raised in an affluent suburb of Chicago. His father was a lawyer, so as a child, Larry was "home-schooled" in law and current events from an early age. In high school he was active in the Civil Rights movement and the student movement to end the Vietnam War; he became a draft counselor before he was eligible for the draft. He trained as a paralegal, and attended Oberlin College in Ohio, where his interests expanded to include Latin America.

After graduation, rather than going to Latin America, Larry joined the Volunteers in Service to America program (VISTA) and worked as a paralegal in a Legal Aid office in Spokane, Washington. Eventually, he moved south to the Willamette Valley in Oregon, where he met people in the Chicano community and became involved with helping undocumented workers. For eleven years he worked other jobs to earn a living, while devoting much of his energy to WVIP and then PCUN. In 1988 he was elected secretary-treasurer of PCUN, a position that he has held for 25 years. Larry plans to step down soon, but he will help provide a smooth transition for a young Latino leader to take over his role. However, he will continue to serve as an advisor to PCUN, and will work on the implementation of immigration reform (when a bill makes it through Congress), particularly on educating immigrants about the legalization process. [319]

PCUN has been particularly influential in the Pacific Northwest, and even has had some influence on the national level, because it "plays above its weight class," according to Larry. Even though it is a relatively small organization in a region that is not very important politically or economically, it has been successful beyond realistic expectations because of its significant connections to a wide variety of movements and organizations. "PCUN is deeply rooted in the labor movement, the farmworker movement, and the immigrants' rights movement," he specifies. "We have deep ties going way back with the LGBT community, we've forged alliances with faith organizations, the student movement, and the African-American community, and many other state and national organizations."

On many occasions, PCUN has been called upon to mediate among a number of different organizations that are working toward a common goal, and one measure of their success is what *doesn't* happen. "When things don't fall apart, it's because PCUN has served as a bridge, has added context and managed to get people to take another look," explains Larry. "I think that is a value that PCUN brings to the table, and it speaks to the importance of making deep connections and seeking the common good." Another value that PCUN offers is its commitment to generosity. "The spirit of generosity is at the heart of PCUN," according to Larry. "César [Chávez] demonstrated that the most powerful force of connection is generosity. PCUN has been very generous with our time, and with the materials we have developed that we allow other organizations to use in order to prepare for the *tsunami*, when millions of people come to our collective doors the day after the president signs an immigration bill."

---

319 For this paragraph and the previous one on Larry Kleinman, I have combined information from my interview with him, from Nicholson's article, and from the PCUN website.

In order to explain how he has bridged the cultural gap between himself and the farmworkers, Larry mentions that he does a lot of listening, an echo of what Susana Rivera-Mills said about "profound listening." In order to communicate, he learned Spanish quickly, and María Chávez-Haroldson (a native speaker, portrayed in a previous chapter) commented that his Spanish is excellent. His interactions with others have not always been positive. Sometimes he has been challenged by workers who question his commitment or his place in the union, but, he explains, "The only thing I can offer the workers is my commitment and my skills, and of course my time. I am not here to make decisions for them, that is not my place. My place is to support them, and I've made the decision to do that. I think that most people who agree with me understand that, and people who don't agree with me have a hard time arguing with that." Obviously he has been valued as a leader, because he has been re-elected about a dozen times. Therefore, Larry serves as a good example of an ally who has made a significant commitment to supporting the Latino community, and who has successfully met the challenge of connecting with people who are different from himself.

### Juan Andrade Jr.,
### President of U.S. Hispanic Leadership Institute

Juan Andrade Jr. is the co-founder and president of the United States Hispanic Leadership Institute (USHLI), a national, nonpartisan organization that promotes education, research, and leadership development. Based in Chicago, USHLI seeks to empower Latinos and other disenfranchised groups by encouraging active participation in the political process, and since 1982 has registered over 2.2 million voters, trained more than 285,000 young leaders, and produced 425 studies on Latino demographics.[320] Juan Andrade is a modest, soft-spoken man who endears himself to the public with his self-deprecating humor. During his acceptance speech for the 2011 Hispanic Heritage Leadership Award, he quipped, "[this award] will give other people another reason to believe that I am one of the most overrated Latino leaders in the nation."[321]

Juan Andrade believes that education is essential to our nation's progress. "One of the biggest challenges facing Latinos is the lack of leadership in our community," he said. "As America turns more and more to the Hispanic community for leaders, we must be prepared to step up and meet that challenge and the key is education."[322] He takes that challenge seriously, since he has earned four graduate degrees himself, and has been awarded six honorary doctorates. In 2011 he became the fourth Latino in history (after César E. Chávez, Héctor García, and Mario Obledo) to be honored by the governments of both the United States and Mexico. Former President Bill Clinton bestowed upon him a Presidential Medal for his "exemplary deeds of service for the nation," and Mexico recognized his contributions to Mexicans and Mexican Americans by presenting him with the Ohtli Award, the highest honor presented to a civilian not living in Mexico.[323]

As a boy, Juan Andrade sold newspapers, picked cotton and hoed weeds in the fields outside his hometown of Brownwood, Texas. During his high school and college years, he labored in

320 USHLI website and Wolfman Productions website.
321 "HHA 2011 Dr. Juan Andrade."
322 "Juan Andrade Jr.," 1/3.
323 USHLI website.

factories and meatpacking plants.[324] After working for some years as a political commentator on ABC-7 television in Chicago and then as a columnist for the *Chicago Sun-Times,* he found his true calling and began giving back to the Latino community. He has broadened his vision of civic engagement to include non-Latinos. "It's important for Latinos to register to vote and to elect candidates of our choice, not necessarily Latinos, but candidates who represent everybody," he explains.[325] In a separate speech, he expands upon this concept: "What we need in this country from the grassroots community all the way to the national level is a whole new generation of agitators, people who can shake things up and make things come clean so we can have a better and more just society for everyone."[326]

USHLI sponsors the largest Latino leadership conference in the nation, and co-sponsors various regional conferences. According to district attorney John Haroldson, who serves as a volunteer group leader at both regional and national conferences, Juan Andrade's speeches at these events have inspired countless Latino youths to embrace their cultural identity and make a commitment to be active contributors to society.[327]

Juan Andrade has expanded USHLI's reach and created international alliances by participating in conferences for the promotion of democracy in at least seven Spanish-speaking Latin American countries, as well as Guyana, Suriname and Haiti. "As leaders we need to take ourselves out of our comfort zone and learn different things outside of our field of work," he explains.[328] This is one of the important lessons of Juan Andrade's life.

---

324 "The Most Decorated Latino Leader in the Nation," 1/1.
325 "Civic Engagement and the Latino Community."
326 "Dr. Juan Andrade from USHLI talks about civic engagement."
327 "Interview with John Haroldson and María Chávez-Haroldson" recorded by Kay S. García on 5 Nov 2012.
328 "Juan Andrade Jr.," 3/3.

# Author activists

In the chapter on Sandra Cisneros, I explained how Sandra combined her writing with socio-political activism, and how her literary works constitute another form of activism. Many authors do this, but Latino writers have done so to a remarkable degree. Perhaps their messages are so urgent that it would seem like a waste of time to produce a purely esthetic work with no social commentary. Latino authors are following the tradition of the great Latin American writers of "magic realism," a literary style that incorporates significant socio-political criticism into works of profound esthetic beauty and complexity. In comparison to works written in nations where multiple forms of peaceful protest are allowed, Latin American literature takes on more significance because it constitutes the only allowable criticism of authoritarian regimes from within the oppressed countries. Latino authors, while not laboring under a dictatorship, have contributed significantly to cultural understanding because of their honest description of life in the margins of U.S. society. For these reasons, I am including one more Latina author (Cherríe Moraga) and one Mexican author (Elena Poniatowska). The latter writer represents another set of allies, the Latin American authors who have inspired and fostered the success of Latino writers in this country.

## Cherríe Moraga,
## Advocate for LGBTQ, Latinos, and Indigenous People

Almost all of the individuals and organizations included in this book have mentioned their support of and connection to the LGBTQ community. Cherríe Moraga is an outspoken member of that community, as well as a person of mixed heritage (Anglo and Latina), and thus she is a good representative of a group of people who have had to navigate through several different layers of discrimination. Kimberlé Crenshaw introduced the concept of *intersectionality* to describe how race, gender, class, sexuality, and other factors (such as age and ability) intersect and affect people's experiences in different ways.[329] Cherríe Moraga has managed to reconstruct her own identity by recognizing and celebrating the multiple dimensions of her experience, and by doing so she has empowered herself and others who find themselves at diverse intersections in the social network. In the seminal work she edited with Gloria Anzaldúa, *This Bridge Called My Back: Writings by Radical Women of Color*, Cherríe refers to her worldview as a *theory in the flesh*:

---

329 Crenshaw 1241-1299.

A theory in the flesh means one where the physical realities of our lives —our skin color, the land or concrete we grew up on, our sexual longings —all fuse to create a politic born out of necessity. Here, we attempt to bridge the contradictions in our experience. We are the colored in a white feminist movement. We are the feminists among the people of our culture. We are often the lesbians among the straight. We do this bridging by naming our selves and by telling our stories in our own words.[330]

Cherríe's story begins in Los Angeles, where she was born with the features of her Chicana mother and the skin of her Anglo father. Since her father was her only Caucasian relative who was present, her mother's extensive family provided the dominant culture in the home. Nevertheless, Cherríe was encouraged to "pass" as white in order to succeed at school and college. It wasn't until after graduating from a small college in Los Angeles in 1974 that Cherríe openly embraced both her lesbianism and her deep connection to her Chicana heritage, an acknowledgement that has profoundly influenced her writing. After working for a few years as a high school teacher, Cherríe moved to San Francisco and by 1980 she had earned a master's degree from San Francisco State. Soon afterwards, she collaborated with the author-activist Gloria Anzaldúa on *This Bridge Called My Back* (1981), a well-known collection of essays, short stories and poems by women of color. Two years later she co-edited the anthology *Cuentos: Stories by Latinas* (1983), with Alma Gómez and Mariana-Carmona.

That same year, Cherríe co-founded the "Kitchen Table: Women of Color Press," to publish works without discriminating by sexual preference, class, or race. Combining social activism with writing, she helped organize women-of-color groups to work against violence, while she published and produced plays that dealt

330 Moraga and Anzaldúa (unnumbered, introductory page).

frankly with race, ethnicity, sexuality, and gender-related issues. She spent time in Boston and New York, but eventually moved back to the Bay Area and became a writer in residence at Stanford University, where she still works. Currently, she lives in Oakland with a partner, and has two grown children. She is a founding member of *La Red Xicana Indígena* (Chicana and indigenous network), which is dedicated to raising indigenous consciousness and supporting the struggles of all the indigenous peoples of the Americas.[331] In the name of the network, the term *Xicana* is used to refer to Chicana feminists.

In the Foreword to *This Bridge Called My Back*, Cherríe directly addresses the practice of using literary works to draw people out of their private circles and into social activism: "The political writer, then, is the ultimate optimist, believing people are capable of change and using words as one way to try and penetrate the privatism of our lives."[332] In the Preface to this same book, Cherríe mentions that her faith helped her keep working on the book, even when she was feeling discouraged. "I'm not talking about some lazy faith," she specifies, "where we resign ourselves to the tragic splittings in our lives with an upward turn of the hands or a vicious beating of our breasts. I am talking about believing that we have the power to actually transform our experience, change our lives, save our lives. Otherwise, why this book? It is the faith of activists I am talking about."[333]

Cherríe describes her own process of empowerment in another contribution to their edited book, her poem called "The welder":

---

331 For this paragraph I have woven together information from a variety of sources, including Cherríe's website, the author bios on her books, an interview, and the websites of the University of Minnesota and University of Illinois at Chicago.
332 Moraga and Anzaldúa, Foreword to Second Edition of *This Bridge Called My Back*, unnumbered page.
333 Ibid. xviii.

"I am the welder./ I understand the capacity of heat/ to change the shape of things./ I am suited to work/ within the realm of sparks/ out of control./ I am the welder./ I am taking the power/ into my own hands."[334]

Sparks fly throuhout Cherríe's sole-authored book, *Loving in the War Years: lo que nunca pasó por sus labios* (what was never said), which was first published in 1983, and then re-issued with a new section in the year 2000. Written in a mixture of English and Spanish, this groundbreaking work combines prose and poetry, and merges personal and family history with political analysis. Besides chronicling her progression from street fighter to zen warrior (figuratively speaking), it serves as an important critical presentation of Chicana/lesbian/feminist thought.[335] Although Cherríe notes significant differences between white feminists and women of color, primarily based on class and ethnicity, her overall message is one of frank discussion for the sake of authentic solidarity: "We women need each other....The real power...is collective. I can't afford to be afraid of you, nor you of me. If it takes head-on collisions, let's do it. This polite timidity is killing us."[336]

There is nothing polite or timid about the eponymous play in *Heroes and Saints & Other Plays*. Cherríe wrote this play in response to the United Farm Workers' grape boycott to protest pesticide poisoning. She dedicated the drama to the legacy of César Chávez, and created one of the characters as a tribute to Dolores Huerta. The main character, Cerecita, was born without arms or legs because of the toxic chemicals her mother was exposed to when she worked in the fields. Cerecita spends most of her time encased in a rolling wooden box, and her caustic commentary reveals uncomfortable truths about society. The community has

334 Ibid. 220.
335 Yarbro-Bejarano. And Cherríe Moraga's website.
336 *Loving in the War Years* 59.

been protesting their high rate of cancer deaths by hanging the bodies of recently deceased children on crosses in the fields, and as public outrage and the workers' dissent intensify, the rhythm of the play accelerates as it leads inexorably to a violent, tragic climax. Thus, Cherríe uses a literary work –both the written and the performed play– to personalize and dramatize the life-and-death issues that farmworkers are facing as they struggle to feed their families.

"We [marginalized people] are often roadkill," she explains in her 2011 collection of writings, *A Xicana Codex of Changing Consciousness*, "the victims of the speed and reckless driving of U.S. greed and racist domestic policies.... Roadkill –those unnecessary dyings of heart, spirit, body—is avoidable if we'd only slow down and learn to walk again."[337] Referring both to her own writing and to the lessons to be learned from elders, Cherríe states, "These are knowings, not imaginings, not stories we tell ourselves to bring comfort to the grieving. Because they do not comfort, they provide energy for hard change and transformation."[338]

As several of the Latino leaders portrayed in this book have pointed out, there is an important link between spirituality and social transformation. In a search for inspiration and guidance for individual and collective change, Cherríe and her collaborator Celia Herrera Rodríguez traveled around the western United States in order to record a variety of indigenous spiritual practices. *New Fire*, the "ceremonial performance" that resulted from their journey, weaves together documentary video and live performance, reveals truth through fact and fiction, and blends history with myth. The central character, a 52-year-old woman, tries to free herself of the toxic residue of violence done to her and to reconnect with her ancestral past. The play connects the suffering of an individual to the suffering of her people and presents a spiritual, feminist and

337 *A Xicana Codex of Changing Consciousness* 66-67, and 72.
338 Ibid. 198.

environmentalist vision of the world. [339]

With few exceptions, the reviews of Cherríe's work have been very positive and scholars have recognized her important contributions to Xicanisma (Chicana feminism) and to Chicano theater. Her writing has received many awards, and she has earned significant funding for her endeavors. Her plays have had successful performances throughout the country. What seems to matter most to Cherríe is her mother's legacy. In the Prologue to a work-in-progress, *Send Them Flying Home, A Geography of Remembrance*, she recognizes her debt to her mother for both the inspiration and the content of her writing. "I am a white girl gone brown to the blood color of my mother, speaking for her," she insists, repeating words she wrote many years ago.[340] Cherríe wishes to keep her mother's culture alive for other Latinos, and she uses her mother's story to combat "cultural amnesia." "Hers is the story of our forgotten," Cherríe explains, "the landscape of loss paved over by American dreams come true. Maybe that's the worst of it, that Mexican dreams can come true in America at the cost of a profound senility of spirit."[341]

Although she usually writes about her mother's culture, Cherríe has not forsaken her father's heritage, and like Sandra Cisneros, she refuses to choose between them. She has created harmony for herself by deciding which aspects of each culture work for her: "If [a particular quality] fits, then that's your business, but if it doesn't fit and it's a source of agitation, [then] it's the agitation that you go to, it's that place that causes you then to be whole, not broken, not in pieces, not half and half but whole—in the way that your spirit calls you to be."[342]

---

339 Derr 1/2.
340 *Loving in the War Years* 60 and 61.
341 Prologue to *Send Them Flying Home, A Geography of Remembrance*, posted on Cherríe Moraga's website.
342 Giarratano 3/4.

218

# Kay (Kayla) S. García

## Elena Poniatowska,
## Mexican Author-Activist and Ally to Latinos

The news anchor Jorge Ramos mentions Elena Poniatowska as someone who inspired him because of her courageous criticism of the Mexican government, while Chicana author Sandra Cisneros expresses her gratitude for Elena's help and encouragement. Elena translated Sandra's first novel, *The House on Mango Street*, into Spanish, and thereby gave it her most heartfelt stamp of approval and made it accessible to millions of readers. Elena has been identified by many critics as one of Mexico's best writers, and without a doubt, she is the most beloved author in that country. Cartoons of Elena show her as an angel, hovering over Mexico City and projecting her glowing light down on the metropolis. Elena has served as writer-in-residence in U.S. universities such as the Five Colleges in Western Massachusetts, and given countless literary workshops and talks throughout the country (in California, Oregon, Nevada, Wisconsin, New York, and many points in between). She has helped train Latina authors, encouraged publication of their works, and spoken out about what Mexican women authors could learn from Chicana writers. She has granted numerous interviews

219

to U.S. scholars, and helped many graduate students and young professors jumpstart their careers.

Elena was born in France in 1932 and immigrated to Mexico with her family when she was ten years old. Her mother belonged to the Mexican upper class, and her father was related to the last Polish king, which earned Elena the nickname "La princesa" (the princess) at the beginning of her career as a journalist. She put that moniker to rest with the publication of *La noche de Tlatelolco (Massacre in Mexico)*, a searing indictment of the 1968 massacre of student demonstrators in Mexico City. The government was severely chastised again in her work *Nada, Nadie* (Nothing, Nobody), which revealed the ineptitude and corruption of officials in charge of rescuing victims of the 1985 earthquake in Mexico City. In both of these works she created a literary montage of multiple sources with different perspectives, including newspaper articles, political speeches, chants and signs held by demonstrators, and the testimony of numerous survivors. These diverse narratives are unified by the author's vision, as she skillfully weaves the pieces together in a "point/counterpoint" pattern, presenting the government's version of events and then providing many direct contradictions to their account.

Elena has published short stories, novels, biography, and interviews, and she has contributed significantly to the genre of testimonial literature, and to the art of the incisive interview. In both her fiction and journalistic writing, Elena has focused on giving voice to women, laborers, student activists, and indigenous rebels such as the Zapatistas in Chiapas. She has been honored with prestigious literary prizes in Mexico, Chile, France, and the United States, and in 2006 she was awarded the Lifetime Achievement Award by the International Women's Media Foundation. After her 80th birthday, she still was traveling around Mexico, the United States, Europe, and even Iceland, giving inspirational talks, attending political demonstrations, and proving by word and by example that a life dedicated to socio-political change is a life well lived.[343]

Elena has interviewed several Chicana authors, including Cherríe Moraga, Gloria Anzaldúa and Norma Alarcón, and she has praised their ability to free themselves of the shackles imposed by society. In a lecture that she delivered at Hampshire College in 1991, Elena asserted that "[Chicana authors] have achieved what Rosario Castellanos asked for in one of her most beautiful poems: a new way of being human and free." [344] She describes how the Chicana writers have overcome discrimination due to class, race, and sexual preference, and, she explains, "From this devastating battle they came out stronger, and have lived in twenty years what has taken Mexican women a hundred years. They are way ahead of us." Elena criticizes the apathy in Mexico toward works written by Chicanos, and states that, "The knowledge of Chicano literature could enrich us in more ways than one, and teach us what it means to fight for freedom, to break down stereotypes, to rescue and demystify the Virgin of Guadalupe in the land of gringos. The liberty with which Chicanas write is an example to Mexican women writers."

Elena refers to writing and publishing as potentially subversive actions, and she celebrates the Chicanas' rebellion against religious dogma, particularly their liberating interpretations of the Virgin of Guadalupe. "Breaking religious canons in Mexico is breaking

---

343 Information in this paragraph comes from numerous conversations that I have had with Elena over a period of three decades, and from the chapter on her in my book *Broken Bars: New Perspectives from Mexican Women Writers*. Some of this same information can be found in Michael Schuessler's biography of her, which is listed in the Bibliography.

344 All quotes in this paragraph are from Poniatowska, "Mexicanas and Chicanas."

cultural canons," she explains. "And political ones. Mexican women are so profoundly marked by religion, the weight of religion is so paralyzing, that the Chicana's absolute will for self-respect and self-assertiveness would be hard for us to accept." After quoting a passage from Cherríe Moraga's book *Loving in the War Years*, in which Cherríe describes how her coming out as a lesbian enabled her to embrace both her sexuality and her Mexican heritage, Elena concludes:

> The [borderland] is fertile and creative, and Cherríe Moraga is right when she says: "There resides in her, as in me, a woman far greater than our bodies can inhabit." To know that we can be greater than our bodies, that we can go farther than our limits, that we can overflow ourselves, are lessons that Chicanas have taught us with their life and literature, and we have not yet known how to thank them.[345]

It often has been pointed out that Latino writers have been influenced by the great authors of Latin America. Elena has demonstrated that it could work both ways, since Latino authors have much to offer Latin American writers. This is a powerful statement, especially coming from such a respected Mexican author. The beneficial connections between Latino and Latin American writers and their works could be enhanced by translations of their books and by presentations at international literary conferences, articles, and workshops on this topic.

Elena Poniatowska's life and publications serve as examples of courageous political dissent and social criticism, expressed in innovative literary texts and tireless participation in public debate, seminars, and workshops. Perhaps an even greater contribution is her recognition of the value and significance of marginalized people,

---

345 All quotes in this paragraph are from Poniatowska, "Mexicanas and Chicanas."

and her ability to give them voice in her writing. Furthermore, she has shown both wisdom and humility by opening her mind in order to discover what she can learn from Latino authors.

The people portrayed in this chapter have demonstrated how making connections and forming meaningful alliances can contribute to positive social change. They have different backgrounds, work in different fields, and operate at different levels of society, but they share a common desire to work toward improving the social order. Some have had a lot to say about activism and leadership, as evidenced by their speeches, interviews, and published works quoted in this chapter, while others have quietly gone about making changes, leading more by example than with words. Henry Wadsworth Longfellow wrote, "Lives of great men [and women] all remind us we can make our lives sublime. And departing, leave behind us footprints on the sands of time." The more footprints there are, the better we will be.

§ § §

## Bibliography by Section

(All web sites accessed Apr-May 2013.)

### Andrade, Juan

"Civic Engagement and the Latino Community." Hartford Foundation video. http://www.youtube.com.

"Dr. Juan Andrade from USHLI talks about civic engagement." Latinos in College video. www.latinosincollege.com.

García, Kay S. "Interview with John Haroldson and María Chávez-Haroldson." Recorded 5 Nov 2012. Unpublished.

"HHA 2011 Dr. Juan Andrade." Hispanic Heritage Association 2011 awards. http://www.youtube.com.

"Juan Andrade Jr." Hispania News website. http://hispanianews.com.

"The Most Decorated Latino Leader in the Nation." Wolfman Productions website. http://www.wolfmanproductions.com/andrade.html.

United States Hispanic Leadership Institute website. http://www.ushli.org.

### Angulo, Eduardo

Angulo, Eduardo. "Change is in the air for public education reform in Oregon." Chalkbloggers website. http://blog.chalkboardproject.org.

---. "Update from the Oregon Alliance for Education Equity (OAEE)." Testimony before the Oregon Education Investment Board. 11 Sep 2012.

"Eduardo Angulo Before Salem-Keizer School Board Meeting." Video by SKCE film group. Ed. and producer Javier Quiroz. Posted 11 Feb 2013 on SKCE website.

"Oregon Alliance for Education Equity press release" (undated). On StatesmanJournal website. http://www.statesmanjournal.com.

Salem-Keizer Coalition for Equality website. http://www.skcequality.org.

### Castro, Julián

Castro, Julián. "Hey Congress: Get immigration reform done." *Politico* website, Sep 4 2013. http://www.politico.com/story/2013/04.

---. Keynote speech at Democratic National Convention, 4 Sept 2012.

Chavets, Zev. "Native Son: Castro at a meeting in January about the rebuilding of the east side of San Antonio." *The New York Times*. 6 May 2010.

Smith, Evan. "Evan Smith Sits Down With...[Julián Castro]." *Texas Monthly*. Vol. 37, Issue 7, July 2009, 64-69.

### Flores, Antonio R.

"Antonio R. Flores speaks at DREAM Act Summit." National Press

Club. 16 Jun 2010. http://www.youtube.com.

"Entrevista Dr. Antonio Flores." Congreso Bienal OUI [Organización Universitaria Interamericana] in Ecuador. 5 Dec 2007. http://www.youtube.com.

Hispanic Association of Colleges and Universities website. http://hacu.net/hacu.

Rivas, Laura. "The 101:The List of the Most Influential Latinos." *The Magazine*, Jul-Aug 2012. http://latinoleaders.com.


### Gonzales-Berry, Erlinda

García, Kay (Kayla) S. "Interview with Erlinda Gonzales-Berry." Recorded 25 Apr 2013. Unpublished.

Gonzales-Berry, Erlinda. *Paletitas de guayaba/On a Train Called Absence.* Trans. Kay (Kayla) S. García and Erlinda Gonzales-Berry. Mountain View, CA: Floricanto Press, 2010.

--- and Marcela Mendoza. *Mexicanos in Oregon: Their Stories, Their Lives.* Corvallis, OR: Oregon State University Press, 2010.


### Gutiérrez, Luis

"Arena Profile: Rep. Luis Gutierrez." http://www.politico.com.

Campo-Flores, Arian. "Keeping Obama to His Word," *Newsweek online*, 29 Nov 2010.

"Luis Gutiérrez Tells Denver Immigrants, Love Yourself, Love Republicans, Too." Feb 2013. http://www.youtube.com.

Luis Gutiérrez's website. http://gutierrez.house.gov.

### Kleinman, Larry

CAPACES website. http://capacesleadership.org.

García, Kay (Kayla) S. "Interview with Larry Kleinman." Recorded 6 May 2013. Unpublished.

Nicholson, Peter S. "Migrant Farmworkers Unite." *Oberlin Alumni Magazine.* Spring, 2000.

PCUN website (*Pineros y Campesinos Unidos del Noroeste*). http://www.pcun.org.


### Moraga, Cherríe

"Cherríe Moraga." Reclaiming History. University of Illinois at Chicago website. http://www.uic.edu.

Cherríe Moraga's website. http://www.cherriemoraga.com.

Cleary, Merideth and Erin E. Ferguson. "Cherríe Moraga." Univ. of Minnesota website, Artist Pages. http://voices.cla.umn.edu.

Crenshaw, Kimberlé. "Mapping the Margins: Intersectionality, Identity Politics, and Violence against Women of Color." *Stanford Law Review.* Vol. 43, No. 6. Jul 1991, 1241-1299.

Derr, Holly L. "New Fire From Cherríe Moraga." *Ms.* Blog. Submitted 11 Jan 2012.

Giarratano, Lisa. "Interview with Cherrie Moraga." *Divisadero* magazine, Spring 2012, University of Southern California website, http://www.usfca.edu.

Moraga, Cherríe and Gloria Anzaldúa, eds. *This Bridge Called*

*My Back: Writings By Radical Women of Color.* 1981. New York: Kitchen Table: Women of Color Press, 1983.

Moraga, Cherríe. *A Xicana Codex of Changing Consciousness.* Durhan & London: Duke University Press, 2011.

---. *Heroes and Saints & Other Plays.* Albuquerque: West End Press, 1994.

---. *Loving in the War Years: lo que nunca pasó por sus labios.* Boston: South End Press, 1983.

Yarbro-Bejarano, Yvonne. *The Wounded Heart: Writing on Cherríe Moraga.* Austin: University of Texas Press, 2001.

### Poniatowska, Elena

García, Kay S. *Broken Bars: New Perspectives from Mexican Women Writers.* Albuquerque: University of New Mexico Press, 1994.

Poniatowska, Elena. "Mexicanas and Chicanas." Lecture at Hampshire College. San José State University website. Submitted 30 April 2004 (link no longer active).

Schuessler, Michael. *Elena Poniatowska: An Intimate Biography.* Tucson: University of Arizona Press, 2007.

### Rivera-Mills, Susana

García, Kay (Kayla) S. "Interview with Susana Rivera-Mills." Recorded 18 April 2013. Unpublished.

Rivera-Mills, Susana and Juan Antonio Trujillo, eds. *Building Communities and Making Connections.* Newcastle upon Tyne, UK:

Cambridge Scholars Publishing, 2010.

Sherman, Lee. "A Place of Belonging." *Terra* magazine. Oregon State University. Winter 2013, 21-25.


**Rubio, Marco**

Grunwald, Michael. "Immigrant Son." *Time* magazine. 18 Feb 2013, 26-30.

Marco Rubio's website. www.rubio.senate.gov.

Parker, Ashley and Jonathan Martin. "Senate, 68 to 32, Passes Overhaul for Immigration." *The New York Times*. www.nytimes.com/2013/06/28.

Rubio, Marco. *An American Son: A Memoir.* New York: Sentinel, 2012.

"Senator Rubio delivers Closing Remarks on Immigration." U.S. Senate Floor Speech. 27 Jun 2013.


**Velázquez, Nydia**

"Nydia M. Velázquez." *NYTimes*. 20 Feb 2013.

Nydia M. Velázquez's website. http://velazquez.house.gov.

# Conclusion

## More leaders, advocates, and role models

This book could have been much longer, but the constraints of time and space meant that numerous people were left out. I would have liked to include civil rights activists such as Jorge Plasencia (chairman of the board of NCLR, the National Council of La Raza), Janet Murguía (president of NCLR), Anthony Romero (gay rights advocate and president of the American Civil Liberties Union), and Sylvia Castillo (director of the National Network of Hispanic Women). In a more lengthy book I would have discussed the work of public health advocates like Aida Giachello, María Gómez, and David Hayes-Bautista.

The entertainment industry supports a lot of people who are working to improve the lives of others, such as María Elena Salinas (co-anchor of Univisión's nightly news show with Jorge Ramos), Cristina Saralegui and María Hinojosa (talk show hosts), César Conde (president of Univisión), and Eddie "Piolín" Sotelo (radio announcer). Many actors have set up foundations and do extensive volunteer work, including Rosario Dawson, Selena Gómez, Eva Longoria, and Edward James Olmos. Latino musicians and artists have made significant contributions, e.g. Lila Downs (musician, patron of the arts), Lilo González (Salvadoran singer, advocate for immigrants), Jorge Rodríguez-Gerada (culture jammer, artist), and Gustavo Dudamel (music director).

The astronaut Ellen Ochoa and the quarterback for the New York Jets, Mark Sánchez, are examples of successful Latinos in other fields who have done community outreach and serve as role models for young Latinos.

230

In the fields that I did cover there are many more people who could have been portrayed, such as the writers Norma Alarcón, Ana Castillo, Denise Chávez, Rudolfo Anaya, and Rolando Hinojosa. The topic could be expanded by including people who are no longer alive, like the writers Gloria Anzaldúa and Tomás Rivera, and the labor organizer César Chávez. If both the temporal and geographic boundaries were expanded in order to encompass all of Latin America -past and present- an abbreviated list might include: writers Carlos Fuentes and Gabriel García Márquez, human rights activists Oscar Romero and Rigoberta Menchú, groundbreaking politicians such as former Chilean presidents Salvador Allende (1970-1973) and Michelle Bachelet (2006-2010), leaders of the Wars for Independence (José de San Martín and Simón Bolívar), leaders of the Mexican Revolution (particularly Emiliano Zapata), and perhaps the revolutionary fighter Che Guevara. Obviously there is a lot more research that could be done on this subject, and once again I find myself having to apologize for the omission of the names of many other talented and notable people.

## Ordinary beginnings, extraordinary outcomes: Shared stories

Rather than being limited by the humble or commonplace circumstances of their birth, the Latino leaders portrayed in this book can be defined by the path they have chosen: a lifetime of service, both as a career and as volunteer work. They all have struggled to define their identities as they have dealt with two cultures, two languages, and two often-contradictory lives: personal and professional. They have defied expectations which were set too low for them or were too restrictive. They have overcome adversity in the form of poverty, discrimination, disease, and physical abuse, and they have transformed their anger into positive action. They have learned that time is precious and should only be spent on issues for which they have a passionate commitment. They have taken advantage of opportunities, learned from failures, and ignored the naysayers.

These leaders managed to excel not only because of their own strength and determination, but also because they had the love and encouragement of at least one adult in their lives, as well as inspiration from important role models. At some point in all of their lives, somebody recognized their talent and encouraged them to study hard and set high goals for themselves. Such mentoring can be life changing, and thus it should be an important component of educational reform, youth programs, and leadership training.

Other traits these leaders have in common are a sense of adventure and a willingness to learn new skills and new ways to have fun. They have a good sense of humor and do not take themselves too seriously, which has helped them withstand the criticism so often directed at them. They are intellectually curious and willing to work hard and make sacrifices for the common good. They all have made important connections to other people and other causes, while several of them have expanded their activism to make global connections.

At the center of their being is a profound generosity of spirit. All of these leaders have expressed great satisfaction in serving their communities and making a difference in other people's lives. Erlinda Gonzales-Berry mentioned that her volunteer work is spiritual because it feeds her soul. Spirituality seems to be one of the factors that made it possible for some of these leaders to persevere under challenging circumstances. Cherríe Moraga calls it the faith of activists: the belief that we have the power to transform our experience. In search of insight and guidance, Cherríe traveled around to record the spiritual practices of indigenous people, and she has shared their collective wisdom through her writing and public performances of her play *New Fire*. Sandra Cisneros has created for herself an image of Buddhalupe, a nurturing and liberating version of the Virgin of Guadalupe. Susana Rivera-Mills tries to incorporate spirituality into every aspect of her life because that kind of integration helps her remain true to her core values. Staying connected to their own forms of spirituality has helped some of these leaders define their identities, make important decisions, and determine the principles that have shaped their lives.

An important source of strength for these leaders has been their commitment to the Latino community. Some of them are still learning Spanish, but they all recognize the importance of the language and have made an effort to retain their cultural heritage. In her memoir, Sonia Sotomayor praises the Spanish language because it can make accessible the beautiful prose and poetry of Latin America and Spain, and it can open a pathway to cultural understanding. In a work in progress, Cherríe Moraga is recording her mother's cultural memories so that the author will not lose her soul. She comments that the American Dream is often realized at the expense of one's spirit. This is an interesting observation, since so many of these leaders' lives have been offered as proof that the American Dream is real and attainable. These leaders have avoided such loss of soul by maintaining close ties with friends and family, returning to their childhood neighborhoods to help others succeed, and giving back to the wider Latino community.

Another problem with the American Dream is that it is not accessible to everybody, particularly not at the level reached by the leaders portrayed in this book. Nevertheless, the journey is more important than the destination, and individuals have made important contributions whether they have helped just one person or many people. The accomplishments of these leaders are not presented as a standard by which to judge one's own life. Rather, these stories reveal that it is possible to make a difference in any setting, and this is the main reason that I have included people who have attained different levels of recognition and success.

## Individual contributions

Sonia Sotomayor used adversity to her advantage, utilizing a diagnosis of diabetes as motivation for making every day count and for being disciplined in all that she does. She is a staunch defender of Affirmative Action as a creator of opportunities for serious students from disadvantaged neighborhoods. She is known for her insistence on the rule of law even in the face of undue pressure, and for her meticulous investigation of all the facts before making a decision. Sonia believes that it is important to realize how her rulings affect people, and for this she relies on the empathy born of her life experiences. She has a history of promoting civil and human rights, and she has dedicated many hours to pro bono activities and training students to become lawyers. Even as Supreme Court Justice, she continues to visit schools and universities to inspire students to work for justice in the legal field or in their chosen profession. She believes that laws have the potential to improve society, and therefore it is important that all sectors participate in the process of making, interpreting, and enforcing those laws.

Dolores Huerta defied all expectations by organizing and contributing to the success of the United Farmworkers Union while raising eleven children. She is particularly well known for her promotion of nonviolence and for her efforts to improve the status of women within progressive movements. She has served as an important bridge between women of color and the Feminist Movement, and has repeatedly expressed her support for women's right to pursue their dreams. Her Weaving Movements campaign encourages all progressive organizations to coordinate their efforts in order to increase their effect on society. At the age of 84, she is still active in the Dolores Huerta Foundation, which encourages civic participation at the grassroots level.

Jorge Ramos has been identified as a new breed of journalist because he combines objective reporting on his daily news broadcast with overt advocacy during his weekly political talk show and in his syndicated columns. The numerous books and articles that he has written about immigration reform provide a human face for the immigrant experience and offer statistics and convincing arguments in favor of transforming the laws. Jorge is broadening the scope of his influence by participating in an English-language news channel for Latinos and others interested in Latino issues. His life story reveals one of the consequences of the censorship of the media in Latin America: the exodus of many talented intellectuals. As a result of his ardent advocacy for authentic democracy in that region as well as his incisive interviews of authoritarian leaders, he has increased awareness of oppressive regimes that claim to be democratic. His shows are broadcast throughout Latin America, and with an audience estimated to be in the millions, he has a significant impact. On the personal side, Jorge has made an effort to stay connected to his children, and he gives them the same advice he offers students who are searching for direction: do what you love, and do it with passion.

John Haroldson and María Chávez-Haroldson provide proof that a mutually respectful relationship can be empowering. Their synergy has made it possible for them to make significant contributions to the Latino community on the local, state, national and international levels. John is working toward making the legal system equitable and accessible, and María is engaged with student groups, protecting victims' rights, and empowering Latina homemakers to take control of their lives. They both contribute to leadership training for Latino youths at the regional and national levels. In Mexico, they participate in workshops to help train judges, lawyers, and advocates for crime victims, and thus facilitate the judicial reform in that country. María exemplifies what women can accomplish when they escape the cycle of poverty and abuse, and John is another example of someone turning a devastating diagnosis into motivation for hard work and service to others. They both demonstrate the concept of paying it forward, sacrificing now so that the next generation can succeed.

The literary works of Sandra Cisneros are a figurative call to arms. Besides presenting a realistic vision of what it is like to grow up in the *barrio*, her writing makes young people think about their lives and the meaning of their existence. She offers them alternatives to society's low expectations and encourages them to use their time on this earth wisely. Both her prose and poetry demonstrate the importance of finding one's own voice based on personal life experiences. In addition to presenting Latino issues to the general reading public, her work presents a feminist perspective within a culture that is often dominated by males. Her short story "Woman Hollering Creek" transforms the tragic and undermining myth of *La Llorona* into a liberating and celebratory tale of redemption. Her activism is not limited to the printed page, since she often speaks to student and community groups and organizes cultural events as well as peace demonstrations. Sandra has created two foundations to foster socially engaged writing and she provides grants and workshops to encourage aspiring writers.

The politicians presented in Chapter Six have recruited allies and formed coalitions in order to make significant progress on a wide variety of issues. They strive to represent all of their constituents and to further many different causes. An impressive measure of the success of Latino politicians is that both major political parties have a potential presidential candidate who is Latino: Julián Castro for the Democrats and Marco Rubio for the Republicans.

In the field of education, students are being prepared to participate in an increasingly inclusive global community through alliances with communities, service learning, and courses throughout the curriculum that address the issues of difference, power and discrimination. Such transformative education is enhanced by engaged research, which increases understanding of Latino communities and other marginalized groups.

Community outreach, labor organizations and leadership training workshops have created bridges between Latinos and non-Latinos and have encouraged active civic involvement. These activities have contributed to the growing web of connections, while attracting even unlikely allies to their cause.

As an author-activist, Cherríe Moraga has eschewed polite timidity by producing plays that deal frankly with race, ethnicity, sexuality and gender-related issues, as well as with pesticide poisoning and other concerns of farmworkers. The distinguished Mexican author Elena Poniatowska has drawn attention to the fact that Latin Americans could learn some important lessons from Latina writers. She praises Latinas for their new way of being human and free, and for going beyond the limits of their bodies. Elena believes that literature can be a form of subversive action, and she uses her writing as both political dissent and social criticism. Moreover, she has recognized the value of marginalized people, and in her books she gives voice to women, laborers, student activists, and indigenous rebels.

### Final observations

Each of the leaders in this book has the potential to influence the reader in a different way. Sonia Sotomayor is serious, Jorge Ramos is provocative, Dolores Huerta is defiant, Sandra Cisneros is sassy, and the Haroldsons are both dedicated to their community and devoted to each other. Perhaps the reader will be encouraged, as I have, to cultivate these qualities within themselves. Readers may be inspired by Susana Rivera-Mills' sense of integrity, Cherríe Moraga's faith of activists, or Larry Kleinman's acceptance of another's cause as his own.

One uncomfortable aspect of these stories is that they clearly illustrate the fact that discrimination takes many forms and affects our lives and our society in multiple ways. Even though these remarkable people have managed to scramble up a slope made slippery by prejudice, that does not mean the climb is accessible to everybody. Community outreach and transformative education provide ways to combat prejudice by sharing with the general public the gifts that Latinos bring to our country. Not only have they contributed to literature, the arts, media, politics, and the economy, but they also have influenced our food, language, music, and entertainment.

The values that many Latinos embrace could be an antidote to the materialism and individualism of American society, since Latinos tend to appreciate people of all ages, particularly children and the elderly, and their extended families often provide vital support and encouragement. Many Latinos have a joyful spirit, piquant sense of humor, and ability to live in the moment, all of which have the potential to enhance the vitality of our collective soul. In recent years Latinos have been stepping into leadership roles, occupying a vacuum created by politicians and other leaders who have burned out or have been pushed out by scandals and ineptitude. Some of the new leaders' stories are presented in this book and perhaps their example will inspire many others so that our society will continue to be energized and renovated by their contributions. Like Sandra Cisneros' character the River, who flows into all the waterways of the world, Latino and Latina leaders of the future will have an effect on everything, everything, everything, everything.

## Appendix

## Transformative Education

"Education is really the only revolution that's sustainable, that lasts and that actually can have an impact, an influence on positive change that is long term," according to Susana Rivera-Mills.[346] She and her colleague Juan Antonio Trujillo have edited a collection of essays that present innovative pedagogical methods for establishing connections with underrepresented communities: *Building Communities and Making Connections in the 21st Century.* In the introduction to this book, Susana explains the need to increase students' intercultural competence by providing opportunities for civic engagement: "Simply sharing space or being exposed to those who are culturally and linguistically different from ourselves is not enough to bring us into intercultural knowledge and understanding. We must engage with the 'other' in a meaningful interaction in order for transformative education to happen."[347]

Susana mentions Learning Communities and service-learning as examples of what she calls "pedagogies of engagement." Learning Communities are interactive groups of students and faculty who meet for large blocks of time in order to explore interdisciplinary themes together in an intense, integrated course. Service-learning requires students to learn about underrepresented communities by interacting and providing some service to them. Service-learning is an important component of Learning Communities, and it also may be integrated into other courses. Susana concludes that "[transformative education and engaged research] is where higher education is headed or should be headed…. As we prepare global

346 García, Kay. "Interview with Susana Rivera-Mills."
347 Ibid. viii.

citizens we must challenge our students to become engaged in civic responsibility and social consciousness in order to successfully effect positive change."[348]

In the conclusion of their edited volume, Juan Antonio Trujillo states that "language and culture professionals are uniquely positioned to play a leading role in the transformation of higher education.... [since] we carry the humanizing touch that is needed to move the academy forward."[349] He describes the transformative educational process as one in which critical reflection and discourse lead to actions that advance equity. In his passage on *curricular transformation* he explains, "A transformed curriculum is one that seamlessly integrates the history, literature, learning styles, and values of populations that historically have been marginalized... ."[350] Juan Antonio Trujillo sees transformative education as an alternative to the market-driven priorities that have shaped traditional curricula: "In the transformed (and transformative) educational environment," he writes, "service is a core value... [and] scholarly activities ... are informed by community needs."[351]

In order to be successful, transformative education needs to be introduced to faculty with a thorough explanation of its philosophical tenets as well as its potential benefits, and faculty need to participate actively in the process of determining specific components of the curriculum.

The creation of Ethnic Studies departments in major universities, which began in the 1970s, has contributed significantly to a general acceptance of a more inclusive curriculum. In order to extend inclusivity to multiple areas of academic instruction, other programs have been initiated, such as the Difference, Power and

348 Ibid. xv.
349 Ibid. 255.
350 Ibid. 252.
351 Ibid. 251.

Discrimination program (DPD) and the Heritage Learners progam. DPD courses encourage students to develop empathy and build coalitions around common causes in order to promote positive social change. In the introduction to *Teaching for Change: The Difference, Power, and Discrimination Model*, Larry Roper and Jun Xing explain that "DPD is concerned with helping students understand the complex dynamics of difference, power, and discrimination and how those dynamics influence institutions, with the goal of empowering students to alleviate oppression and other negative outcomes."[352]

In an essay included in the above mentioned book, Susan M. Shaw and Annie Popkin describe how to facilitate a seminar to prepare faculty members to develop and teach DPD courses and to utilize innovative, interactive teaching methods. Rather than simply adding material written by marginalized groups to their syllabi, professors are taught how to move issues of difference and power to the center of the content and teaching processes. The seminar addresses the important issue of how to transcend individual experiences of oppression in order to see others as allies. "We go over the fundamentals of active, engaged listening and speaking," explain Susan Shaw and Annie Popkin, "looking for connection, noticing disconnects and examining barriers to listening. The seminar provides a practice space for democratic teaching."[353] Thus, the seminar provides a support system for curricular transformation and also serves as a microcosmic example of an alliance based on solidarity across differences.

Another example of transformative education is the Spanish for Native Speakers program, also known as Spanish for Heritage Language Learners, which has been developed in many universities as a means to address the specific needs of Latinos who speak Spanish at home but do not have formal training in the language.

352 Xing, Li, et al viii.
353 Shaw and Popkin 76.

These courses give students an opportunity to explore and affirm their bicultural identities, and they often provide life-changing experiences for both faculty and students. "I was transformed by the personal experiences of my students. I was broken and remade," declares Loren Chavarría, the founder of Oregon State University's Spanish for Heritage Language Learners Program and co-creator of the Advanced Spanish Learning Community.[354] Loren Chavarría explains that both SHLL and ASLC provide opportunities to place the experience of U.S. Latinos at the center of the curriculum. "For years we have been teaching Spanish as a 'foreign language' in this country," she writes. "Now we are changing the focus in order to encourage our students to learn Spanish in order to *serve* the Spanish-speaking community at the university, in the community, in the state, and eventually in the entire country. In this way we are participating consciously and actively in the promotion of social justice by means of individual transformation."[355]

One of her students, Eder Mondragón Quiroz, said that he discovered his calling as a bicultural psychologist by taking one of Loren Chavarría's courses:

> The class was oriented toward understanding the culture and students' own experiences, [and toward] understanding what it means to be a Spanish speaker in the U.S.... I started to understand I wasn't alone in feeling the pull between my Mexican and U.S. identities. There were other bicultural people who shared my experiences of living 'in the margins.' I hope to get the opportunity to use that understanding to support younger generations of Latin@s with struggles they may face.[356]

---

354 Quoted in Carillo 20.
355 E-mail from Loren Chavarría, translated by Kay S. García.
356 Quoted in Carrillo 20, and e-mail from Eder Mondragón.

Such testimony provides a glimpse into what is happening in classrooms across the country and shows how education can be transformed in order to foster sustainable, positive change in society.

§ § §

## Works Cited

Carillo, Celene. "Telling and hearing the stories: How personal narrative transformed Eder Mondragón Quiroz into a leader." *Oregon Stater.* Spring, 2013, 18-22.

Chavarría, Loren. E-mail sent to Kay S. García. 25 Jun 2013.

García, Kay S. "Interview with Susana Rivera-Mills." Recorded 18 Apr 2013. Unpublished.

Rivera-Mills, Susana and Juan Antonio Trujillo, eds. *Building Communities and Making Connections.* Newcastle upon Tyne, UK: Cambridge Scholars Publishing, 2010.

Shaw, Susan M. and Annie Popkin. "Teaching Teachers to Transgress: Facilitating the DPD Seminar." *Teaching for Change: The Difference, Power and Discrimination Model.* Xing, Jun and Judith Li, Larry Roper, and Susan Shaw, eds. Lanham, Boulder, New York, Toronto and Plymouth, UK: Lexington Books, 2007, 67-110.

Xing, Jun and Larry Roper. "Introduction: Difference, Power and Discrimination (DPD), Social Justice, and Curricular Reform." *Teaching for Change: The Difference, Power, and Discrimination Model.* Xing, Jun and Judith Li, Larry Roper, and Susan Shaw, eds.

Lanham, Boulder, New York, Toronto and Plymouth, UK: Lexington Books, 2007, vii-xii.

# Kay (Kayla) S. García
## Author's Biography

**Kay (Kayla) S. García** is Professor of Spanish in the School of Language, Culture and Society at Oregon State University. She was born in Wisconsin, but she lived in Mexico for seven years and in Spain for two years. She has a BA, MA, and PhD in Spanish and an MA in Latin American Studies. She is the author of *Broken Bars: New Perspectives from Mexican Women Writers* (UNM Press, 1994) and translator of the following literary works:

*Cloud for Sale!* translation of Elena Poniatowska's children's story, "La vendedora de nubes." Bilingual edition. Floricanto Press, 2013.

*Mourning for Papá: A Story of a Syrian-Jewish Family in Mexico*, translation of the novel *Los dolientes* by Jacobo Sefamí (Plaza y Janés, 2004). Floricanto Press, 2010.

*Paletitas de Guayaba/On a Train Called Absence.* Bilingual edition of a novel with the translation by Kay S. García and the author, Erlinda Gonzales-Berry. Floricanto Press, 2010.

*When I was a Horse and Other Stories.* Translation of short stories by Brianda Domecq. Fort Worth: TCU Press, 2006.

*The Astonishing Story of the Saint of Cabora.* Translation of the novel *La insólita historia de la Santa de Cabora* by Brianda Domecq. University of Arizona: Bilingual Press, 1998.

*Eleven Days.* Translation of the novel *Once días...y algo más*, by Brianda Domecq. Albuquerque: UNM Press, 1995.

64390337R00148

Made in the USA
Lexington, KY
06 June 2017